A FRENCH MAP OF THE ISLES OF THE CARIBBEES AS KNOWN IN 1688, BASED ON THE WORK OF COSMOGRAPHER PERE CORONELLI OF VENICE.

Isles of the
CARIBBEES

by Carleton Mitchell

FOREWORD BY MELVILLE BELL GROSVENOR
President and Editor, National Geographic Society

PREPARED BY NATIONAL GEOGRAPHIC
SPECIAL PUBLICATIONS DIVISION
Robert L. Breeden, Chief

NATIONAL GEOGRAPHIC SOCIETY
WASHINGTON, D.C.

ISLES OF THE CARIBBEES
by Carleton Mitchell

Published by
The National Geographic Society
Melville Bell Grosvenor,
President and Editor

The third in a series of National
Geographic books from the Special
Publications Division.

Gilbert M. Grosvenor,
Editorial Director

Robert L. Breeden, *Editor*
Donald J. Crump, *Assistant Editor*
James S. Cerruti, *Manuscript Editor*
Philip B. Silcott, *Assistant to the Editor*
Johanna G. Farren, *Research*
Michael E. Long, *Picture Editor*
Joseph A. Taney, *Art Director*
Josephine B. Bolt, *Assistant Art Director*
Ronald M. Fisher, *Production*
Luba Balko, *Production Assistant*
James R. Whitney, *Engraving and Printing*
Editorial Staff: Bruce Brander, Tadd
    Fisher, Mary Ann Harrell, Geraldine
    Linder, Cynthia Ramsay, Linda Seeman,
    Gerald S. Snyder, Peggy Winston;
    Margaret S. Dean, *Assistant*

Wind-driven spray drenches *Finisterre* as she pitches in choppy seas on
an island passage. Author Carleton
Mitchell holds the liferail for balance.
Overleaf: Rainbow arcs above the
cruiser-racer off Petit Piton, a sailors'
landmark on verdant St. Lucia.

JAMES STANFIELD (RIGHT) AND NATIONAL
GEOGRAPHIC PHOTOGRAPHER WINFIELD PARKS (OVERLEAF)

Foreword

THIS BOOK was born on blue water. Fresh trades were pushing us across Anegada Passage in a rhythmic rush. I was standing watch with skipper Carleton Mitchell on his 38-foot yawl *Finisterre* during his cruise from Grenada to St. Thomas.

Mitch felt like talking. And because he is a truly great storyteller, I shared the mood. Our conversation ranged as wide as the sea: modern ports and vanished pirates, rich plantations, shipwrecks, fine meals and fishing trips, sea battles, sudden storms.

"Wonderful yarns!" I said at last. "Mitch, you have to write another book!"

His earlier *Islands to Windward*, after seven printings, is still a classic among lovers of the West Indies. Now he must reach a whole new public; his book must guide not only the jet-age tourists but also the yachtsmen who are cruising there in their own and chartered boats. More than that, this book should be a guide for those questing spirits who would use it as their passage to one of the world's most romantic regions.

Finisterre's log may not record the hour this book began, but now as I leaf through the pages I can all but hear Mitch's voice, and taste the salt of ocean spray.

There's Brimstone Hill towering upon St. Kitts. We climbed it at dawn, that "Gibraltar of the West Indies." From the 750-foot summit, we admired a dazzling view of bright channels and the isles of Statia and Saba. And then our friend Lt. Col. Henry Howard, Administrator of St. Kitts, told us the story of the islands' turbulent past.

Angered by the Dutch salute to the new U. S. flag at Statia in the year 1776, British Admiral Rodney sacked its rich port—seizing many ships and stores of British and St. Kitts' merchants. Retaliating, Colonel Howard told us, the Kittitians refused to help British troops carry cannon up to Brimstone Hill Fort in the face of an impending French attack. We could almost see the 1,200 defending Redcoats—and imagine their despair when their own guns below were turned against them by the 6,000 besieging French. The British fought bravely before finally surrendering.

With Mitch, I tried skin diving for the first time. And I must admit that my undersea view of the shipwreck *Rocas* was one of the eeriest experiences of my life. This freighter, sunk on Horse Shoe Reef around 1929, still carries a grisly cargo: the bones and grinning skulls of horses.

On Peter Island, we explored that pirate haunt Deadman Bay and the desolate cay named Dead Chest. One view of the bleak setting, and my favorite sea chant took on new meaning: "Fifteen men on the dead man's chest. . . ." By tradition, Blackbeard left mutineers stranded here.

Such are the rich details that bring glamour to forgotten rocks and make history breathe anew. Here is the whole West Indies—as varied as Europe, with its isles so strongly French, Dutch, English.

Only Carleton Mitchell could have done this volume. He writes as he sails—intensely, with great order and flair. We would cruise all night, Mitch navigating, standing his watch, and skippering to boot. Then at dawn he would go ashore to spend the day interviewing people, collecting notes.

I also admired the skill of National Geographic Photographer Winfield Parks, who could do his trick at the helm—and take superb pictures at the same time. And all of us owed a debt to Henry Davis, our sailor friend and gifted cook who fueled us for prodigious labor.

Later, another crew turned to here in the Society's headquarters. Assistant Editor James Cerruti worked closely with author Mitchell; and Robert L. Breeden, Chief of the Special Publications Division, with his talented staff, ably steered the editorial course for *Isles of the Caribbees* in the wake of *Finisterre*.

Finally there is *Finisterre* herself. I have admired that sleek craft since she did the seemingly impossible by winning the Newport-to-Bermuda race three times in succession. It is my pleasure to welcome each reader aboard this worthy winner.

Melville Bell Grosvenor

Tinged with gold by early-morning sun, fishing nets swing from drying poles on Martinique. Islanders

Contents

using seines like these reap the sea's harvest off uncounted beaches throughout the isles of the Caribbees.

I *Grenada:*
Gateway to the Windwards

Cloud-shadowed hills cradle anchorages at St. Georges's, capital of Grenada. From this "Spice Island of

M<small>ANY YEARS AGO</small> I had a dream that came true, with reality more pleasant than the dream. When I was a boy the Caribbee Isles captured my imagination. As I sailed landlocked Lake Pontchartrain, near my native New Orleans, at an age when most small neighbors were intent on shooting marbles, I could suddenly see a wake lying white against blue water astern, feel hot sun and cooling trade wind on bare shoulders, and over the bow visualize green palms and shadowed mountains. Someday, I vowed, I would navigate my own boat through the Windward and Leeward Islands of the West Indies.

Whenever I came across a map of the area I would run a finger along the dots that curve north from the shoulder of South America like the pearls of a beautiful necklace. As I read every book on the area I could find, the men who had pushed back the horizon became real to me—the whole incredible streaming of life from the Old World to the New—explorers, colonists, traders, soldiers, priests, and buccaneers.

Of all the figures who wove a tapestry of romance with their keels, none seemed as great as the first, Christopher Columbus. He wrought superhuman feats of seamanship despite human frailties and the superstitions of his era. Yet there were others whose names rolled down through history like mighty ocean swells from the past.

Pierre Belain, Sieur d'Esnambuc, planted the fleur-de-lis under the tropic sun. Peter Stuyvesant lost a leg in a battle off St. Maarten before going on to that more northerly Dutch settlement, Nieuw Amsterdam.

the West," author Carleton Mitchell began a ten-week cruise of the Windward and Leeward Islands.

PAINTING BY HEINRICH BERANN

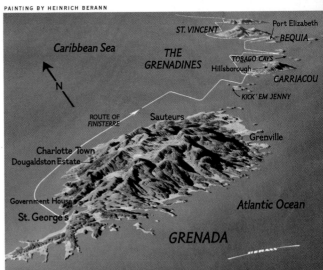

The Elizabethan freebooter Sir Francis Drake gave his name to the channel in the Virgin Islands through which he passed to attack San Juan in 1595; and that other famed freebooter, Sir John Hawkins, died on the same expedition and was buried at sea. Later came other naval heroes, names to conjure visions for every boy: Hood and Rodney and Horatio Nelson.

Then too there were the early inhabitants, the Caribs, whom Columbus called "Indians." The accounts I read of this savage people fascinated me. No Spartan child ever endured such privations and trials in his training as a Carib warrior or fought more bravely as a man.

When taken, "they did no more put off their fierceness and cruel countenances than do the lions of Libya when they perceive themselves to be bound in chains," wrote historian Peter Martyr in *De Novo Orbe Decades*, published in 1516. "There is no man able to behold them, but he shall feel his bowels grate with a certain horror."

I sailed and studied through the years, pushing back my own horizons, always thinking of that someday cruise. Finally, in 1947, I embarked. Poking through the islands in a ketch named *Carib*, I found

Foaming crest smashing across her foredeck, the author's 38-foot yawl *Finisterre* demonstrates her power as she drives to windward in steep offshore seas. Grenada (map, above) is southernmost of the 250-mile-long Windward chain.

11

NATIONAL GEOGRAPHIC PHOTOGRAPHERS WINFIELD PARKS (ABOVE) AND DEAN CONGER

Sunlight and mace flow through skilled fingers of women grading the aromatic spice in a plant at Charlotte Town, on Grenada's leeward coast. Mace grows as a ruby cloak on ripe nutmeg (left); if unbroken when removed, the fibrous cover brings a higher price. Workers (right) crack nutmeg shells and sack kernels for export. Grenada's volcanic soil also produces cloves, cinnamon, cacao, and fragrant tonka beans.

an interweaving of races, languages, and customs against an island background of surprising variety in contour and character —even climate. My dream had indeed become reality.

Then came a period of preoccupation with other things and places. Yet always there lingered in my mind memories of drowsing fishing villages and colonial capitals, roofs peeping through the palms, as well as the warm hospitality of remote communities. I knew I would go back, and yet I feared that what I had found and loved on that first trip might no longer exist.

"The West Indies have changed," I was often told. "Direct jet airliners to major islands only a few hours from New York, Paris, or London, and shuttle planes on to the smaller cays. Fancy hotels. Hard to locate a deserted beach."

Now, 18 years later, I was returning to sail my 38-foot ocean cruiser-racer *Finisterre* in the wake of *Carib*. I had chosen Grenada as a starting point, planning to retrace the island-hopping migration of the Caribs. Variously called Caribs, Charaibes, and Caribbees in old accounts, they were a

12

mysterious people who once lived in the Amazon jungles of Brazil.

Not long before the arrival of the first Europeans they came out of the Amazon country to flow northward by canoe, overcoming an earlier people, the less warlike Arawaks, devouring the males captured in battle and taking their women. One spelling of the Caribs' name, *Caniba,* gives us the dread word "cannibal."

By the time Columbus arrived on his second voyage in 1493, the Caribs had reached the Virgin Islands, where they were stalled by the sheer number of Arawaks on the large land mass of Puerto Rico.

THOUGH the Caribs' poisoned arrows met Columbus on his second voyage — rather than the hospitality accorded him by the Arawaks on his previous landfall in the Bahamas — it was the Caribs who gave their name to the sea. The Spaniards exterminated the Arawaks in the islands, but the Caribs resisted for centuries — and the spark is not yet extinguished, as we were to find on Dominica.

I had sent *Finisterre* ahead, and as I flew to Grenada to pick her up, doubts assailed me. Would I find that the tropic languor and the sense of mañana had been swallowed by the pressures of the 20th century?

Peering down as I neared my goal I had my first reassurance. Seas rolling unchecked from Africa splintered against a coast almost as untamed as the ocean itself. The plane dropped over an escarpment to land on a pocket-handkerchief airfield that ended at Atlantic shallows.

Soon a taxi was taking me up the steep spine of the island on a highway dating from the days of French ownership.

As we climbed, lush vegetation pressed in from both sides. Waxy dark green leaves of breadfruit alternated with the delicate tracery of coconut-palm fronds. Poinsettia and bougainvillea added splashes of color. Then came uplands almost perpetually damp from enveloping clouds. Suddenly after the blazing sunshine of the beach I was chilly, wrapped in cloud mist as penetrating as New England fog.

The road was better suited to the produce-laden donkeys we passed than to the trucks we saw. "This banana-ship day," explained my driver as we crawled along behind a towering load of green stems topped

Oyster-white sand of Grand Anse Beach slips through shadowy coconut palms to the sea, welcoming cooling trade winds and inviting a stroll by children with pet goats. A smiling girl reflects the warmth of her island in the sun.

NATIONAL GEOGRAPHIC PHOTOGRAPHER WINFIELD PARKS

14

by a boy playing his harmonica. "They's takin' they fruit to St. George's to sell. Here we got no minerals and not many visitors. We got to grow things to eat."

For miles we drove through forest broken only by occasional clearings and huts. Then we went over a final crest to see the Caribbean shimmering far below, and I glimpsed rooftops as the road wound down through cultivated plots. Nearing the coast, I was almost reluctant to enter the streets of St. George's. It existed in my memory as the perfect small West Indian town. Since my last visit Grenada had been devastated by a hurricane, and then there was all that progress I had heard about.

I need not have worried. I found a town as unmistakably tropic-colonial as a pith helmet—perhaps a bit more populous and prosperous than before, with more modern shops, but basically the same.

A turn brought us to the open-air market, always the pulsing heart of a simple community. I knew that the women behind the displays of fruit and vegetables had arrived at dawn. Some had brought their wares in large baskets balanced on their heads; others had squeezed into the island buses—flatbed trucks with homemade bodies and wooden planks for seats.

In the market square, also the bus station, I alighted to find fancifully painted vehicles with even more fanciful names— Creole Pride, Angel Guardian, Take-it-Easy, and One More—this last perhaps referring to the capacity, as it always seemed possible to find space for another passenger.

I became part of the market's remembered swirl of color and smell and sound. Around me upended boxes and trestle tables displayed not only exotic tropic produce but also the familiar staples of the temperate zones. Among mounds of breadfruit, mangoes, pigeon peas, and bananas, I found carrots, potatoes, onions, tomatoes, and corn. Children scampered underfoot, dogs barked, and tethered chickens pecked at scraps fallen from the tables. Knives

15

flashed as vendors lopped off tops of coconuts for thirsty shoppers. Piles of dried fish looked like stacked firewood.

A dark hand extended three golden oranges. "Here de best, mistah," called a voice in the softly slurred accents of the islands. "De mon want bananas," interposed another vendor. "Look yere, sah!"

"Look, sah," became a chorus, and soon I had filled a coconut-fiber basket. I paid fractional prices by most standards, using "BeeWee," the official currency of the British West Indies. A B.W.I. dollar was then worth about 70 cents U. S.

St. George's begins at the seashore with Bay Town and flows over a roller-coaster hill to Carenage Town, which rims a harbor that is the flooded crater of a dead volcano. In 1895, engineers pierced the hill with a tunnel, but citizens and visitors alike prefer the streets, with a glint of water at each end.

As I topped the rise, I saw the fortress that still guards the port, cannon pointing above the Caribbean in defiance of white-winged fleets whose bones have long lain among the coral. Sloops and schooners moor at a horseshoe quay lined by shops and warehouses, and the hillside beyond makes a green backdrop crowned by the gingerbread majesty of Government House.

"The Windward Islands haven't altered much," His Honour Ian G. Turbott, C.M.G., C.V.O., Administrator of Grenada, told me later as we sat on the terrace of Government House. "Ours is still an agrarian economy, based on exporting tropic produce to northern overseas markets. Life on the plantations goes on pretty much the same. Tourism is now becoming a factor, and of course forms a great hope for the future. Yet most visitors stay close to their hotels, basking on the beach and leaving the life of the people basically unchanged—so far."

In planning my cruise, I had been confused by a multiplicity of names referring to the area. On his first voyage, ending in the Bahamas, Columbus thought he had

NATIONAL GEOGRAPHIC PHOTOGRAPHER DEAN CONGER

In a tug-of-war with the rolling surf, fishermen on Grenada's Grand Mal Beach haul in a seine heavy with sharp-nosed bait-fish called ballyhoo (below). Thrusting above newly planked fishing schooners, coconut palms bend to trade winds that blow almost ceaselessly among the emerald-green islands of the West Indies. Warm waters of the archipelago also yield dolphin and bonito.

arrived at an archipelago off the China coast. He referred to the islands as *Las Yndias Ocidentales* — the West Indies.

Renaissance cartographers, remembering the legendary lost land of Antillia, showed the islands on some maps as the Antilles. Accordingly, Puerto Rico and the larger islands to the west became the Greater Antilles, and the eastern islands the Lesser Antilles.

Early Spanish navigators made their division in terms of the prevailing breezes. Those eastward, in the teeth of the trade winds, were *Islas de Barlovento*, the Windward Islands. Those downwind (off the coast of South America) were *Islas de Sotavento*, the Leewards.

The English upset this logical division when they acquired most of the islands between Grenada and Puerto Rico. For ad-ministrative purposes, they split them into two groups, the Windwards and the Leewards. But in terms of prevailing trade winds, the British Leewards lie to windward of the Windwards!

"The dividing line between the two groups of colonies shifted many times through the centuries," Administrator Turbott said when I asked him to help me sort out the terms. Dominica, southernmost of the Leewards, is administered as part of the Windwards. As a further complication, the Dutch call their northern islands (northeast of Curaçao) — Saba, Sint Eustatius, and Sint Maarten — the Netherlands "Windward Islands," although they lie among the British Leewards!

In theory, the Caribbean became a Spanish lake soon after its discovery. In 1494, the Treaty of Tordesillas, based on papal bulls of Alexander VI, divided the non-Christian overseas world between Spain and Portugal. Spain received all territories west of a line drawn through the Atlantic Ocean at approximately 50 degrees longitude, which gave it not only the islands but also North and South America.

The other maritime nations of Europe scoffed at the division. Soon the English, French, Dutch, and Danes were sailing almost where they pleased. Spain eventually lost control of the Caribbean. In 1624 the first English colony settled there on St. Kitts. Rival nations quickly staked out colonies, and for two centuries played a game of musical islands to the tune of cannon fire against a background of diplomacy.

Leaving Government House, I taxied around the commercial port of St. George's. This brought me to a new inner harbor created by dredging a channel across a bank that had barred entrance to a natural lagoon. Virtually stormproof, with a marina and repair facility, the sanctuary is a fine example of the development that aids the islands most. *Finisterre* lay there snug and jaunty among other floating nomads.

I had first conceived *Finisterre* as a miniature home afloat, sufficiently sturdy to cross an ocean, yet shallow-draft enough

Raven-haired carnival queen Christine Ferguson swims in sparkling water below Annandale Falls near St. George's. Ferns peek from the spray and philodendrons climb the rocks.

through use of a centerboard to enter teacup harbors. A yawl rig divided her sails into units one man could handle, while such electric aids as an automatic pilot and powered anchor windlass eased chores on deck. Below, her design for living included a refrigerator, a shower, and a coal-burning fireplace for colder climes. A stove and table gimbaled to remain level in rough weather ensured comfortable meals. Shelves of books and a hi-fi tape system provided pleasure while at anchor.

When *Finisterre* was launched at Saybrook, Connecticut, in 1954, my sailing friends shook their heads dubiously. Only 38 feet 8 inches on deck, with a waterline length of 27 feet 6 inches, against a beam of 11 feet 3 inches, my dream ship looked like a ripe watermelon. "She won't be able to get out of her own way," was the verdict; but soon her virtues as a cruiser were obscured by her fame as an ocean racer.

Her victories included two Miami-Nassau Races, and three consecutive and unprecedented "firsts" in the Newport-to-Bermuda classic. Yet wanderings as a cruiser had carried her as far as the Mediterranean Sea. And now she awaited me in the St. George's marina.

Standing on deck was Henry Davis, philosopher and wit, fellow veteran of midnight battles with flogging sails. Many thousands of miles we had put astern together, including two transatlantic passages. A sailor who had given up the sea to work in a Maryland shipyard, Henry could not resist my suggestion that we take another cruise together aboard the boat we loved. Capable of doing any job and cool in any emergency, Henry not only would keep *Finisterre* in trim, but also would liberate me for unworried exploration ashore.

The third member of the crew was to be Winfield Parks of the NATIONAL GEOGRAPHIC photographic staff. One of his first pictures to gain fame was of the 1958 America's Cup defender *Columbia*. Thousands of photographs were taken that summer, yet Win's came closest to capturing the way of a boat with the sea.

Grenadian on a slalom ski skims a wake off St. George's. Island waters lure deep-sea fishers, skin divers, and yachtsmen. Children born to the sea swim as easily as they sprint the sands.

While no sailor, Win soon learned to take his turn at the wheel and helped as much as any man could, defying the seaman's motto: "One hand for the ship and the other for yourself." In Win's case, it was frequently one hand for the ship, one for a camera, and only an eyelash for himself!

We had arrived in time to celebrate Old Year's Night, Grenada's way of saying New Year's Eve. Henry had been aboard since Christmas, listening to music rolling down the hillside as the musicians practiced. "Have you ever heard a steel band playing carols in calypso rhythm?" Henry asked, preparing me for the evening's "jump-up," local slang for a dance.

That evening while friends in the north shivered in the cold, we sat on the terrace of the Spice Island Inn and heard weird but compelling music issuing from an assortment of junked auto parts and oil drums. As the stars revolved overhead,

tempo and volume increased, until the whole island seemed floating on the waves to a jungle beat.

When Grenada returned to an even keel, I found that the biggest change since my last visit was due to the passage, in 1955, of the evil lady named Hurricane Janet. The Grenadians had considered themselves out of the hurricane belt, as storm centers usually pass to the north.

"Nobody heeded the warnings," I was told by Mrs. Clive Belizaire, who lives near Government House. "At seven on the evening of September 22, the Governor came on the radio to say the eye of the storm would pass over St. Vincent, and asked us to pray for the people. Then, instead of hitting St. Vincent, the storm struck us on Grenada at nine. Our strongest winds came at about eleven, when the front door blew in as the back door blew out. All our windows went. A tree crashed on the roof. My

Smiling grandstand belles chat excitedly during a race at Seamoon Track near Grenville, on Grenada's eastern shore. Railbirds at left crowd the infield fence to watch their favorites pound past the starter. Island-bred horses race at Seamoon and at Barbados and Trinidad tracks.

husband and I crouched under our heaviest table in four inches of water.

"Many roofs from the houses on the slope below ended in our yard. People kept coming by asking if I had 'seen a red roof,' or 'a green roof,' and I'd say to go look, we had plenty to choose from!"

Now, in contemporary island history, events are fixed in time as happening before or after *The* Hurricane. Janet flattened or washed away countless huts, stripping whole hillsides, and leaving 137 dead. "Grenada was like a plucked chicken," said a survivor. "Everywhere you looked at bare earth. You saw things you never knew were there."

When I visited Dougaldston Estate, one of the largest plantations, I realized what such a disaster meant to a people depending on the products of slow-growing trees.

"We lost almost 80 percent of our po-

tential cacao production," said William P. Branch, manager since 1908, a spry gentleman of 82.

We passed aromatic vats where cacao beans "sweat" away a fibrous outer covering under a blanket of banana leaves. Mr. Branch explained, "Before the storm we made 1,200 bags; in 1956 we shipped 180. Ten years later, we are only back to 700 bags. Our nutmeg and mace production suffered even more. Most of our trees were blown down. Only the females produce, and it is five or six years before a nutmeg tree 'declares' by putting out blossoms. Then male trees must be removed, and bearing females spaced—it takes 15 years in all to reach full output."

To the credit of the islanders, few scars are visible today. Grenada again deserves the title "Spice Island of the West." I saw the growing and processing of cacao, nutmeg, mace, cloves, and pimentos, as well

Forbidding needles of the prickly-pear cactus *(Opuntia)* guard fragile blossoms that rival the brilliance of the setting sun. Sweet-scented frangipani (above) blooms in clusters, its overlapping petals curling at the edges. In Latin America, bougainvillea (left) often takes the name *trinitaria* because three showy bracts cup each tiny flower.

as experimental plantings of coffee, vanilla, and black pepper. I found, too, that between tree and table there's many a step in the preparation of island exports.

Cacao, for example, when picked looks like a small melon. A cutlass—that multipurpose swordlike knife of the West Indies whose name evokes pirate days—splits the cover open. The beans, held by clinging fibers, are imbedded in a white pulp, from which fermentation, or sweating, removes them. Plunging my hand in a vat, I found an uncomfortable damp heat, much higher than body temperature.

The cacao beans then are sun-dried in large shallow trays, which can be slid under cover if rain threatens. "Stirring women" shuffle barefoot through the trays to turn the beans for drying, and sometimes the process becomes a dance, to the rhythm of clapping hands. Finally the beans, polished by tumbling in a drum, are hand-sorted for size and quality, then bagged.

Inescapably the aroma of spice is woven through my memories of the island. In nearby Charlotte Town, at a cooperative nutmeg processing station, a large building was piled with sacks awaiting shipment. But here the sound was almost more intriguing than the smell.

After stripping away the outer covering of mace—a valuable spice in its own right—the workers break the hard shell of the nut to get to the "meg," exactly as if extracting the meat of a pecan. Women sat on the floor tapping nuts with uncanny speed and precision, each blow of the mallet a tiny sound; yet the cumulative effect was like a clatter of castanets.

Though Columbus sighted Grenada on his third voyage, he did not stop. It was just as well, for the fierce Caribs inhabiting the island would not have welcomed him. With poisoned arrows, they drove off the first English attempt to land in 1609. The French, however, founded a settlement in 1650, acquiring the island with gifts of knives and trinkets, and—the one thing the Indians found irresistible—two bottles of brandy for the chief. But fighting soon began and the French declared war.

Driving the west coast road beyond Charlotte Town, I topped a rise toward the northern end of the island and came upon the last stronghold of the Caribs, Morne des Sauteurs, or Caribs Leap, with sides dropping sheer to the sea. In 1650, in a surprise raid, French attackers surrounded a council of Caribs on the summit of the cliff. Musket fire blocked the Indians at every turn. Finding their position hopeless, the warriors threw their women and children over the edge, and then made the jump themselves rather than surrender.

I remembered Morne des Sauteurs clearly from my first visit, a windswept point looking out over the smaller islands of the Grenadines, where *Finisterre* would soon carry us. Again I had tea with the priest in his home next to a stone church and walked the cemetery on Caribs Leap, but this time it seemed less somber. Near the church a school was building, a gift of the Canadian Government, and already children were playing there.

On Grenada, as on all the islands, children are everywhere—torrents of children. The population explosion has arrived, partly a reflection of better sanitation and medical care. Schools, medical facilities, housing, and employment opportunities, though expanding, cannot keep pace with a population increasing at a compound interest rate of well over 2 percent—when 3 percent means a doubling in 23 years.

Pulp of a cacao pod hides beans that will become chocolate after workers ferment them in "sweating sheds," then spread them in the sun to dry. Five million chocolate trees grow on Grenada.

23

Deckman Henry Davis can cook as well "with the boat on her ear as when she's straight up," says author Mitchell. Weights in the free-swinging gimbaled stove and table keep them horizontal even in a rolling sea. Lunch here includes French bread, shelled cold crayfish, and a mixed dressing of mustard and mayonnaise.

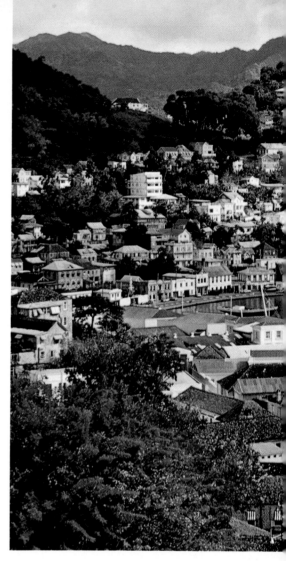

Finisterre **slips seaward** in a morning breeze from

At the same time, islanders everywhere are moving closer to self-government. In 1958, the West Indies Federation was organized in the hope of achieving both a common government and a stable economic bloc. It dissolved four years later when Jamaica and Trinidad withdrew. The smaller islands have since reverted to the former system, except that the Queen's representative has the title of Administrator rather than Governor, and the possessive word "British" has been deleted from references to former colonies. "Colonies" is also a word to eschew—since the islands are now preparing for independence.

"My duty is to invite the leader of the party commanding the most votes after each election to become Chief Minister,"

Administrator Turbott explained. We sat in the high-ceilinged dining room of Government House, built in 1852, when young Queen Victoria ruled an empire on which the sun never set.

Royalty had been entertained here, and ermine-robed figures looked down on us from portraits on the walls. "The Chief Minister then advises me whom he prefers in his cabinet for such posts as Minister for Education, or Trade and Production, and I appoint them. The running of the country is in their hands. I am an adviser, and only occasionally anything more."

Yet as the islands move closer to independence, Britain still grants financial aid and still buys their produce, sometimes at preferential rates. In 1964, Grenada

St. George's harbor. Racer as well as cruiser, she claims victories in three Newport-to-Bermuda classics.

received B.W.I. $1,500,000 to underwrite the budget deficit, and an equal sum for improvement and education.

What will happen when the mother country no longer rules the islands? The day is not far away; the children insist they prefer to walk alone. But as I mentioned earlier, the islanders continue to have children at a staggering rate, intensifying the already formidable problems of housing, subsistence, and employment.

For a small island, Grenada offers great variety in topography and climate. Some 12 degrees north of the Equator, it never knows winter in the northern sense, and winds blowing almost constantly across the North Atlantic keep it free of the stifling equatorial heat of summer.

Above St. George's lies a crater lake called Grand Etang. Often enveloped in cloud, it is like a freshwater pool of the north latitudes. Yet only a few miles away, Point Salines, the southwestern tip, is a desert of sere wiry grass and cactus, bordered by beaches of white sand on one side, black volcanic sand on the other.

Everywhere I found the same hospitality that I had known on my first visit, and life still moved at a pace of mañana. Water taxis skimmed leisurely across the harbor to save pedestrians the long walk around, while donkeys remained the taxis of plantation paths. At night the sound of distant steel bands echoed down the valleys.

The arrival of a banana ship was always a day of fête, with estate workers riding in

25

atop loads and gaping at shop windows.

Sailing out of St. George's, I put my finger on an association that had puzzled me since my arrival. Looking back, I saw the pocket of blue water sheltered behind a jutting peninsula topped by a stone fortress; a rim of pastel houses and green hillside formed a colorful backdrop. Suddenly it came to me that St. George's was a Caribbean version of Portofino, my beloved port on Italy's Mediterranean coast.

Strangely, fate had made the bond between the towns deeper than superficial resemblance. On board as a guest was Charles ("Laddie") McIntyre, Commodore of the Grenada Yacht Club. Sitting beside me, he pointed to a statue just off shore, a bronze figure standing with upraised arms.

"It was a gift to the people of Grenada from the owners of an Italian ship," he explained. "One Sunday morning in 1961 we were starting a race off the club when we heard sirens and hooters. Suddenly smoke rose from the sea. We forgot our race around the buoys to race to the cruise ship *Bianca C*, which had anchored the evening before. By the time our little sailboats got there, along with every other craft in the harbor, the ship was being abandoned.

"Fire had followed an explosion in the engine room. It spread so fast many escaped with nothing but the clothes they were wearing. Our people cared for over 600 survivors until another ship could be sent to pick them up. Grenada received the statue in appreciation."

As he spoke, *Finisterre* drew near the figure, and I recognized it as a replica of the famous Christ of the Deep, which stands submerged off San Fruttuoso—almost in Portofino's front yard.

Outside the harbor we drifted northward along Grenada's western shore. The Caribbean lay unruffled under us. *Finisterre* was encountering a characteristic of West Indian cruising, the lee calm, caused by the wind shadow of the mountains. In these latitudes breezes are almost always from the easterly quadrant, the trade winds which wafted commerce and passengers from Europe to the Americas during the age of sail. On the Atlantic side, and in open channels between the islands, winds are likely to be strong and seas boisterous.

Turning on our small auxiliary engine to push us to the breeze, I let the automatic pilot steer and lounged beside Laddie McIntyre in the cockpit as he shelled pigeon peas for dinner. Charlotte Town slipped astern and Morne des Sauteurs came abeam, and still no wind.

"Maybe it just isn't blowing today," I said impatiently.

Laddie squinted at the clouds above the peaks, paused a moment, and looked at the sea ahead. "Wait," he advised with a grin.

FRED WARD, BLACK STAR

Caribs Leap: In 1650, Carib warriors attacked by the French hurled their women and children into the sea at Grenada's northern tip, then jumped after them rather than surrender. Dominican Father Paul Demajo strolls near the cliff, site of St. Patrick's Roman Catholic Church.

Christ of the Deep: A bronze replica of the underwater statue off San Fruttuoso, Italy, stands in St. George's harbor. The gift of Italian shipowners, it expresses gratitude for the care Grenadians gave survivors of a vessel that sank nearby in 1961.

II *The Grenadines:*
Of Sailors and the Sea

Kick 'em Jenny: Pounded by boat-swallowing currents, the rock north of Grenada lives up to a bellicose

SUDDENLY, as we cleared Grenada, a mighty gust struck us and *Finisterre* lay over on her side as though pushed down by a giant invisible hand. Off went the motor. Whitecaps began to march; as *Finisterre* came alive, spray flew aft like salted rain, drenching us in the cockpit.

Even in cruising trim, *Finisterre* retains her feel of liveliness and power. This was what she had been built for, to slash through ocean swells with never a worry to her crew. Size is not a deciding factor in seaworthiness; lifeboats survive after the steamer has foundered. Rhythmically her sharp bow sliced each oncoming wave, while astern plumed a long lane of foaming wake. Blue water below, blue sky above, and green islands beckoning ahead — none of us would have traded places with any man.

Soon over the jib appeared Kick 'em Jenny, a rocky islet in the Grenadines. "Nobody knows where the name comes from," said Laddie McIntyre. "Maybe it's a corruption of the French, *cay que gêne*, 'the troublesome cay,' because the currents around it gave the old sailing ships such a

nickname. Sailors say the waters kick like a mule around the cliff, called Diamond Islet on some charts.

TED SPIEGEL, RAPHO GUILLUMETTE (ABOVE) AND NATIONAL GEOGRAPHIC PHOTOGRAPHER DEAN CONGER

With leather palm and stout linen thread, a Bequia islander reinforces the edge of a canvas sail.

hard time. Some say it's Kick 'em Jenny because it kicks like a mule; others claim you can see a donkey in the shape of the rock."

To find out, we tacked in close. Around the base of the desolate islet, water creamed white, while seabirds rose from crevices and screamed at us. But no donkey in the rocks, no kick of watery heels for *Finisterre*. A cloud drifted above, the breeze dropped, and we swept past without breaking stride.

Perhaps the least known but among the loveliest of the Windward Islands, the Grenadines have no airports, no easy means of access—only roving yachts, and a waddling diesel mail boat, whose passengers share the deck with produce and livestock.

More than 100 islands and rocks scattered along a submerged ridge extend 50 miles between Grenada and St. Vincent. The southern islands come under the

Hillsborough Bay curves into seven-mile-long Carriacou, largest of the Grenadines. Formerly a

Reef-rimmed lagoon of the Tobago Cays afforded *Finisterre*'s crew an ideal stopover for water-skiing.

jurisdiction of Grenada, the northern under St. Vincent, with the dividing line slicing across the northern tip of Carriacou.

So simple is the view of the world held by many of the isolated residents of Carriacou that they often refer to nearby Grenada as "the mainland." Yet Hillsborough, with electric lights, taxis, and a small hospital, is a relatively sophisticated metropolis, and I had selected its lovely bay as our destination for the night. But as *Finisterre* rounded the final point we had a sudden warning of things to come.

Swells curled into the anchorage. Where normally the water off the beach lay smooth, breakers ran hissing across the sand to wash the base of the palms.

Hillsborough is an open roadstead — not a landlocked harbor but a crescent-shaped bay exposed to swells from the north.

prosperous sugar producer, the dot of land now exports limes, grown by many of the isle's 7,000 people.

NATIONAL GEOGRAPHIC PHOTOGRAPHER WINFIELD PARKS

When trade winds are light and seas small, open roadsteads can be pleasant anchorages. But after a spell of fresh winds, boats roll uncomfortably in the swells.

We backtracked around the point to drop anchor in Tyrrel Bay, near a cove known as the Carenage. Stemming from the term "to careen"—to heave down a sailing ship to work on her bottom—a carenage is a sheltered pocket where a helpless vessel will not be at the mercy of the weather.

No sooner had *Finisterre* dropped her hook than a boat put off from shore, an old friend waving from the stern. He was J. Linton Rigg, former yacht broker, ex-member of the War Shipping Administration, and one of the all-time greats of ocean racing. Linton had retired on Carriacou after exploring the Caribbean. The island had no place for visitors, so he opened a six-room hotel, the Mermaid Tavern, on the Hillsborough waterfront, then built his home, Tranquillity, high on a windward slope.

The next day, as I entered Tranquillity,

I closed behind me a gate bearing a quotation from *A Midsummer Night's Dream:* "Weaving Spiders Come Not Here." We gazed over waving palms to green and blue shallows as brilliant as stained glass. Two small cays, Little Martinique and Little St. Vincent, lay at the edge of soundings, and beyond stretched the open Atlantic, dappled by drifting trade wind clouds. There was no sound except the sigh of the breeze. As we lunched on the terrace, Linton talked of his neighbors, the fisher-folk and farmers of Windward, the village hidden under the palms below.

"When I had my housewarming party, the whole village of Windward attended. We started with Big Drum dances, sometimes called 'nation' dances, because they originated with tribes, or 'nations,' in Africa. Indoors, the older women prepared a feast. They asked me what my mother and father—both had been dead for some time—would like to eat and drink. I thought a minute and said maybe a cup of

NATIONAL GEOGRAPHIC PHOTOGRAPHER DEAN CONGER

"A living mariners' museum," the author says of Bequia, where islanders pursue whales in small boats reminiscent of the golden age of Nantucket. With harpooners braced at the bow thwarts, crews begin the chase when lookouts atop the hills signal on sighting the pluming spouts of their quarry. After a successful hunt, the entire population shares the catch. Bequians (left) beach a 30-foot craft. The whalers (below) load a harpoon gun sometimes used by the hunters, though most prefer to "dart the iron" by hand.

tea for my mother and a glass of rum for my father, then some soup and roast fowl.

"Later, I went in and found a table set for two, with exactly the things I had specified. They told me it was the 'parents' plate,' which couldn't be touched until daylight, and an old woman called a *gan-gan* was set to watch. At midnight all the women gathered. Half sang in patois, 'Who is this food for?' and the other half chanted, 'For good people who are no longer here on earth.'"

I learned more about the islanders from District Officer Wilfred A. Redhead. "It is amazing how our people have retained their identity," he said. "We have descendants of the Ibo, Moko, Temne, Mandinka, Chamba, and Kromanti tribes, brought from Africa more than two centuries ago, and there isn't a man among them who doesn't know what 'nation' he belongs to."

Along with other holdovers from the past goes a practice of magic and sorcery called obeah, not unlike Haiti's more publicized voodoo. At the center of this island

TED SPIEGEL, RAPHO GUILLUMETTE

lore is the legendary loup-garou, a were-wolf that assumes different forms to drink the blood of its victims. Generally it flies like a bat, but sometimes it rolls along the ground as a ball of fire.

In Grenada, Dr. Jan Slominski, a Polish refugee physician decorated by the British Government for his work during the hurricane of 1964, told me an amusing story about this as we sat in the yacht club. "When I first arrived and made my rounds, I noticed the windows of the houses were always tightly shut at night, which I thought bad for the health. But then I noticed that many windows bore painted red crosses. I decided the people were health-conscious, after all, paying such a tribute to our work — until I discovered the red crosses were there to ward off loup-garous!"

Although not officially admitted to exist, obeah is practiced in some form on every West Indian island I visited. M. G. Smith discusses it in a study entitled *Kinship and Community in Carriacou*, published by the Yale University Press in 1962. He writes of "'dealers,' who sell human souls to the Devil, and 'door-openers,' whose spells allow them to enter where they will."

In island lore, the female counterparts of loup-garous live among their neighbors by day but at night become witches who roam abroad seeking sleeping victims, especially fat tender babies. *Diablesses*, cloven-hoofed sirens inhabiting the Grenadian wilderness and the empty cays and rocks off Carriacou, destroy the men they enchant by driving them mad.

Obeah is a phase of local life that goes on below the surface, unsuspected by casual visitors, yet sometimes accounting for behavior puzzling to an outsider. Once I had a maid who would not carry salt to the

Careened for caulking, a sloop lies on her beam ends in Admiralty Bay, Bequia. Block and tackle heaved

table; mothers hiring local girls as babysitters are horrified to return to a room almost hermetically sealed; and I've heard of cases where healthy people sickened and died for no known medical reason. Strange coincidences occur on this island where witchcraft is a part of everyday life. It is said that the one Grenada schooner launched without the blessing of an obeah "doctor" promptly ran onto a reef.

In 1656 a visitor to the Grenadines wrote, "The most beautiful of all the little isles is *Kayryoüacou*," and for me that is still true. The view from the peak above Carriacou's Hillsborough Bay is superb. Palms overhang a double curve of white sand, almost as perfect as though inscribed by two sweeps of a compass, and the water of the anchorage shades through tones of blue into the azure of the Caribbean.

Gone are the camels imported during the 18th century as beasts of burden, but oddities still exist, among them oysters that grow on trees. One morning two local boys rowed us deep into the Carenage, where mangrove trees put their roots down through shallow salt water to the earth below. The boys lifted submerged branches to the surface and harvested the heavy encrustation of shells with broad sweeps of their cutlasses.

Our next goal was the Tobago Cays, a few miles to the north and east of Carriacou, a cluster of uninhabited cays lying in a semicircular lagoon formed by a barrier reef. As we entered, I ignored the chart to con *Finisterre* from the bow by the color of the water ahead. Coral patches showed up as purple-brown smears, and channels as dark blue lanes, paling into green nearer shore. Off the beaches the water was so transparent that I found it hard to tell where dry sand began.

"Port a little — starboard a little," I called aft to the helmsman as we threaded past two small islands to anchor off a third. From deck nothing seemed to lie between *Finisterre* and the open sea, but then to my ears came a distant roaring, and on looking through binoculars I could see Atlantic

her down in shallows as *Finisterre* anchored nearby.

swells lifting, rolling, then breaking against hidden reefs.

When we felt that we were securely anchored we piled into a Boston Whaler to make a circuit of the lagoon. Before we left Carriacou, by pre-arrangement, the mail boat had delivered this fiber-glass tender, stable and seaworthy. It was to make a great difference in our cruise. With its 40-horsepower outboard motor, the Whaler gave Win a camera platform and helped us in exploring coastal waters.

Now in the Whaler we cruised the lagoon, getting a closeup of surf dashing against the coral, and afterward water-skied, snorkeled to look for lambis (the succulent mollusk called conch in other parts of the West Indies), and finally walked beaches as remote as Robinson Crusoe's. We found few footprints. Although the Tobago Cays

sometimes provide shelter for a cluster of cruising boats, we were alone.

After two days of idyllic solitude among the cays, Port Elizabeth, thirty miles to the north on the island of Bequia, seemed almost a metropolis. Finding the wind funneling strongly into Admiralty Bay as we rounded the point, we flattened sails and zigzagged in a series of stairstep tacks. Our Whaler followed on her long nylon painter like a dog on a leash.

Bequia is a true island of sailors and the sea; not of the mechanized vessels of today, but of the past, when sail was the only way to transport people and cargo.

Ashore I met sailmakers on benches in the shade of almond trees, plying palm and needle on canvas and tarred manila, not synthetic fabrics. Nearby, shipwrights swinging adzes faired timbers, putting a

Frenzy of the dance whips the skirt of a Carriacouan while a drummer moans to the beat, his face contorted with emotion. One of several Big Drum dances performed for such occasions as marriages and boat launchings, the Belair enlivens a celebration after a day of feasting. Some islanders, following ancestral ways, practice obeah, sorcery similar to the voodoo of Haiti.

vessel together on the beach. In the shallows, a crew was careening a schooner by block and tackle attached to her mast; they shouted in unison as they hove on the lines, until they exposed one side all the way to the keel for caulking and repainting.

AT FRIENDSHIP BAY on the southeastern coast, I stepped into a living mariners' museum. On the beach whaleboats balanced on bones of their prey, lovely double-ended craft straight from the golden age of Nantucket, with the old-time cutout in the bow thwart to steady the harpooner's knee. Bequia remains one of the few places where men still pursue and capture whales by hand.

Harold Corea, member of a whaling family, tended a vat of boiling pitch. In a long house roofed by palm thatch were stacked oars and harpoons, and neatly coiled line lay in tubs, ready for running.

"Whales begin to come through in February," Harold told me as he tossed bits of driftwood on the fire. "Starting in March and running until summer, four boats will go out every day, six men to a boat. Last year wasn't so good. We got the iron into three, but caught none. The year before we took a humpbacked cow, very big, maybe 65 to 70 feet long, and also her calf."

Whale vertebrae and other bones from past catches decorate one of the most unusual dwellings I ever visited. As *Finisterre* tacked toward Port Elizabeth, I saw a natural stone arch, without noticing that anything lay beneath it. But when we returned in the Whaler for a closer look, I found that the rock arch was probably the world's largest picture window.

37

"Moonhole just happened," its designer and owner, Thomas G. Johnston, told me. He had spent 25 years as an advertising executive in Chicago and New York, and then "suddenly awakened on a Monday morning—in spring—fed up with existing simply for a better job and bigger bank account." He and his wife, Gladys, came to St. Vincent, gravitated to Bequia, and discovered the natural bridge that later became part of their home.

"Moonhole is the local name for the formation because in some lights the round opening in the hillside glows like a full moon," Tom said. We sat on the terrace, protected from a shower by the stone arch overhead; it formed not only a roof but also a spectacular frame for Admiralty Bay and the blue Caribbean beyond.

"We at first intended to build a picnic house, but it grew stone by stone. Being inexperienced in architecture, I didn't

know what I couldn't do. The first masons quit because I wouldn't let them build in straight lines—I wanted to continue the natural forms of the boulders. They thought rooms should have four walls, and none of ours has more than three.

"Our guest room has only one masonry wall, on the entrance side to hang a door for privacy; two of its other sides are the solid rock of the cliff; the arch overhead is the ceiling—and in front there is nothing but the sea and the sky."

Moonhole rambles along the slopes as though it were an outcropping of the rock. In the guest room a tree sprouts from the floor, and one of Tom's proudest moments was when a hummingbird felt so at home that she built a nest and raised two babies.

Flotsam and jetsam form many furnishings and decorations. Fishnet floats—bubbles of glass in cocoons of tarred line—drifted over from Europe and now hang above the dining terrace. Rusted anchor chain brought up from the harbor bottom loops between rock pinnacles as a railing to keep unwary visitors from tumbling into the sea. Whale rib bones form the handrails of steps, and vertebrae have been fashioned into chairs and low tables.

Only the kitchen is modern, but as we sat down to lunch Gladys Johnston pointed to a battered refrigerator against a rock wall. "Even our freezer carries out the motif of free form and the sea," she laughed. "It was knocked out of shape being landed through surf on a rough day."

As we walked down to the beach Tom Johnston said, "The island authorities are trying to give me a road but I don't want it. I'm only a half hour from town by boat, and I'm never in more of a hurry than that. It isn't a case of escapism, it's simply that I like this way of life better than any other I've known. But we're not hermits—come back and see us anytime. If all our rooms are full, we'll make another one for you!"

NATIONAL GEOGRAPHIC PHOTOGRAPHER WINFIELD PARKS

"More a way of life than it is a home," retired advertising executives Thomas G. Johnston and his wife, Gladys, say of Moonhole, their Bequia refuge. Fitted to the cliff beneath a vault of rock, the house has thirteen free-form rooms. For cruising and transportation, the Johnstons maintain a small fleet of their own—a 33-foot ketch, two whaleboats, and three dinghies, usually moored in a cove on the other side of Moonhole's narrow neck of land.

III *St. Vincent:*
The Planter Isle

Palms crowd the sea on St. Vincent, island "horn of plenty" that pours forth a rich bounty of coconuts.

BEQUIA CHANNEL is notoriously rough. When I passed that way before, in *Carib*, I had been told that a watch was kept over small boats by a lookout in Fort Charlotte, and a cannon fired if one capsized. Now we left Admiralty Bay in company with a husky slab-sided schooner that had double-reefed her mainsail, and two fishing canoes of a design so ancient that local lore claims the underslung bow stems from the rams of Carib war canoes.

Three men were in each cranky splinter, along with a pile of gear, so that the boats appeared to have no more than an inch of freeboard, with only that width of planking showing above the surface.

As *Finisterre* ran off before the wind from Port Elizabeth, all was peaceful, but I wondered what would happen when our little fleet rounded the point. For 3,000 miles trade winds blow uninterrupted across the Atlantic, generating long rolling seas and a surface drift.

Arriving at the Windward Islands, the drift funnels into the Caribbean through the passages between, causing a mighty piling up on the Central American coast. This mass of water seeking a normal level finally results in the Gulf Stream as it escapes between Cuba and Yucatan.

A strong current gripped *Finisterre* as we cleared Admiralty Bay, causing steep

bananas, sea-island cotton, and arrowroot. Horses bred for racing graze a deep carpet of pangola grass.

"Like George, with courage dauntless, We may all our foes subdue," sing marching parishioners on St. George's Day. In Kingstown, capital of St. Vincent, scouts (right) step to the tempo of the Royal Police Force band in the Anglican procession. The ceremonial closes in a cathedral named for St. George, patron saint of England. Above, white lace frames the faces of young girls from rural parishes. Two clergymen flank the Rt. Rev. Harold Grant Pigott, Lord Bishop of the Windward Islands. Wearing a delicately embroidered miter and brocade robe, he grasps a crosier, a symbol of his office.

cresting seas through which we drove as spray flew. In the four-mile channel separating us from St. Vincent, the bottom drops to more than 200 fathoms, a great trough of turbulent waters. Yet I need not have worried about the tiny fishing canoes.

Hoisting lace-curtain sails, the crews perched on the weather rails as unconcerned as city dwellers riding in a taxi. When we passed, it was a case of now-you-see-'em-now-you-don't as they swooped over crests and disappeared into the troughs. As we neared a canoe which had dropped her sails to fish, a crewman waved casually and flipped a dolphin aboard.

Standing at the weather shrouds, I was struck by the rich green of St. Vincent's mountains and valleys. From every wave-crest the pattern of cultivated fields became more pronounced, ranging from shore to cloud line. The wind was northeast, forcing us to beat our way through rough seas. A first long tack took us below Kingstown, but when we passed the road-stead I could see the anchored schooners rolling and plunging to the swells. Beyond was a more secure cove off the Aquatic Club, and there we dropped anchor in the shelter of a small islet.

Soon, with Kenneth Punnett as my guide, I saw St. Vincent from a different perspective. Driving up the mountain slopes, I looked down on the regions of Greathead and Mesopotamia, tropical horns of plenty that widened and deepened as they spilled toward the sea which would carry their produce to distant lands. Terraced hillsides and the carefully tended plots of island farmers alternated with large estates. Although I was to find all the Windward Islands rich in the bounty of nature, St. Vincent remains for me the true planter isle.

I could not have had a better guide than Kenneth, a member of one of the oldest families on the island, settlers "since the days we fought the Caribs and the French." Eighteen years ago I had met Arnold Punnett, patriarch of the clan, and once again I

PAINTING BY HEINRICH BERANN

"The true planter isle," author Mitchell calls volcano-crowned St. Vincent. Fields and forest clothe its slopes from shoreline to summits.

Sails snugly furled, a ketch lingers in Cumberland

found him the same courtly gentleman in a starched white linen suit. After graciously receiving me in his home, he sent me forth with Kenneth to meet other relatives.

Thus I came to know Buccament Valley, locally called Punnett Valley. Five members of the family live on its slopes in rambling houses set in frames of tropical flowers, surrounded by lands which form their heritage and livelihood. From the front porch of our first stop, Cane Grove Estate, near a foundation stone dated 1797, I looked over massed banana plants with the owner, John Punnett, who told me:

"Until a few years ago the chief crop of St. Vincent was arrowroot. Then in 1954 the price of bananas went so high they became known as 'green gold.' Planters converted their fields, and the export of arrowroot slipped from 50,000 barrels to 30,000 in 1962. Then, because of rising costs and labor problems, we stopped growing sugar, and much cane land was put into arrowroot. Production doubled in two years. But there was a catch — American manufacturers, our biggest customers, had shifted during the shortage to cornstarch substitutes. So bananas are still our major export."

Later we walked through a banana field, and I learned more of the cultivation of the fruit which is the basis of the Windward Islands' economy. "There are many special terms in banana culture," John said. "The original bearing tree is called the 'mother.' After reaping, it is cut down, and a new trunk, called a ratoon or 'follower,' grows from the roots. There can be several ratoons, but here at Cane Grove we plow up the field and replant after the third."

Stopping at a tree bearing an unusually heavy stem, as bunches are termed in estate parlance, he showed me the hands that grow in clusters. Each banana is a finger. "Planting in rows spaced 8 feet by 4 feet allows 1,360 trees to the acre," he said. It was a staggering statistic. I visualized whole valleys lush with the waving leaves and budding stems of green banana plants.

Later, at a party at Government House on nearby St. Lucia, Sir Garnet Gordon, Chairman of the Board of Geest Industries, Ltd., gave me even more staggering statistics.

Bay. Here amid the palms boys greet visiting yachts with the beat of steel drums fashioned from barrels.

In 1964 alone, Geest ships carried to the British Isles an astronomical 11,731,733 stems, each averaging 120 fingers.

Afterward, sitting in the cockpit of *Finisterre* with paper and pencil, I figured this would add up to almost one and a half billion bananas! And this from Grenada, St. Vincent, St. Lucia, and Dominica alone, not counting neighboring Martinique and Guadeloupe, whose crops go to France.

The richness of St. Vincent's soil played a part in the drama of the Caribs. In 1660, the English and French in a rare spirit of accord and magnanimity agreed the island should remain in the Indians' possession. But, drawn by the promise of lush crops, colonists kept coming. Records as early as 1740 show exports valued at £63,625.

Again, in 1748, Britain and France, in the Treaty of Aix-la-Chapelle, reaffirmed a neutral policy toward St. Vincent, St. Lucia, Dominica, and Tobago. But the agreement was soon scrapped. Intermittent fighting between the Caribs and the settlers on St. Vincent turned into a full-scale war, and a British force finally subdued the Caribs in 1773 after a bloody campaign.

The victorious colonists confined St. Vincent's surviving Caribs to a reservation on the flanks of Soufrière, a volcano on the northern end of the island, and forced the chiefs to sign a document stating: "We ... do swear ... that we will bear true allegiance to his Majesty George the Third ... that his said Majesty is rightful Lord and Sovereign of all the island of St. Vincent, and that the lands held by us the Charaibes, are granted though his Majesty's clemency."

To commemorate the event, a special silver medal was struck showing Britannia

45

Late afternoon sun lengthens shadows on terraced Dorsetshire Hill above Kingstown, where in 1793 Capt. William Bligh put ashore the island's first breadfruit saplings. Other plantings followed, and today the "free-lunch" trees shade many island dwellings.

Rolling surf and driftwood divert island children innocent of bathing suits. On Biabou Beach (right) a girl roves a scalloped stretch of volcanic sand. Miles of empty beaches sweep St. Vincent, where few vacationers call.

Bounty mutiny, Bligh was sent again in command of H.M.S. *Providence*. This time all went well. Bligh anchored off Kingstown on January 23, 1793, and put ashore 544 plants which had been transported from Tahiti. This is a third generation 'sucker,' or shoot, from an original root."

Today breadfruit thrives on the island, but the experiment had unforeseen side effects: Why work when dinner grows just outside? A short time before I had seen a woman walk from her door, knock down a ripe breadfruit with a bamboo pole, and go back to her cooking fire.

In my travels about St. Vincent, I was impressed by its beauty and variety. The cultivated terraces running up the Mesopotamia hillsides reminded me of Italy's Riviera. Lush palm groves flowing down to the leeward beaches, with the roofs of huts peeping through, seemed like the South Seas. The wild windward coast, where long Atlantic rollers crashed against cliffs topped by scant grass and wind-pruned trees, was straight from the shores of Scotland. The belfry of a tiny chapel glimpsed through heavy sea mist and a town called Argyle, which Win and I guessed was probably named for Argyll by a homesick Scot, completed the illusion.

ON THE WINDWARD SIDE Win and I lunched at a plantation where the crop is coconuts—8,500,000 of them in 1964. To get there we drove along a seaside road which narrowed to a trail as the last settlement dropped behind. The earth and beaches looked like packed coal dust as a result of the fallout from Soufrière, whose last eruption in 1902 preceded by one day the disastrous explosion of Mont Pelée on Martinique.

Finally we came to Rabacca Dry River, a miniature canyon sliced into Soufrière's flank. Unseasonable rains made it belie its name, and a stream flowed between jet black walls. At first it seemed we would need the Whaler to cross, but Win waded ahead to find the depth not too great.

presenting an olive branch to a naked Carib, with the inscription "Peace and Prosperity to St. Vincents." Such was the early march of empire.

Because of St. Vincent's fertility, a botanic garden was established in Kingstown in 1765, the first in the Western Hemisphere. One of its purposes was to introduce exotic and commercial plants from the Far East to the West Indies. As we walked through the gardens, the agricultural officer in charge, Conrad de Freitas, showed me many specimens that had come from afar to thrive, and also a spectacular native, the cabbage palm. With its slim straight trunk soaring some 150 feet, its crown of fronds seems to brush the clouds. But the most interesting tree was a historic breadfruit.

"This breadfruit grew from a sapling brought to St. Vincent by Capt. William Bligh," he told me. "He sailed on the *Bounty* to introduce the plant from the Pacific to these islands; the planters wanted it as food for their slaves.

"When the project failed because of the

48

NATIONAL GEOGRAPHIC PHOTOGRAPHER WINFIELD PARKS

Behind this rushing moat, Orange Hill Estate exists as an almost feudal community. After meeting Cyril Barnard, manager and part owner of the plantation, we drove through groves of towering palms where women gathered fallen coconuts into piles for men to husk. I watched workers seize basketball-size nuts firmly in both hands and slash them down on sharp spikes between their knees. Within seconds they had removed the tough outer fiber and passed the inner nut along for the next step, which women performed in the estate's processing area. Lightning strokes of "cut-lasses" halved the nuts, allowing the liquid to flow into tubs.

"After the women remove the coconut meat from the split shells, it goes into hot-air dryers for 17 hours," Mr. Barnard explained. "It will come out as copra—65 percent of it is oil—used for soap, shampoo, margarine, or suntan lotion. Nothing is wasted. The outer husks fire our furnaces, the fluid is given to pigs, and the meal left over after pressing is good for feed for

other stock. Charcoal made from the shell is used in gas masks."

The workers of Orange Hill live in rent- and tax-free cottages built by the estate, and are provided electricity generated by diesel engines. The community is almost self-sufficient, with a school, carpenters, masons, and mechanics; it raises its own cattle, poultry, vegetables, and fruit.

Set on a rise looking across waving palms to the sea, the estate house seemed to embody the charm of the tropics. One end of a long veranda was screened to form an aviary for birds of brilliant plumage. Fan-shaped openings above doors let the trade winds blow through high-ceilinged rooms. Shelves of gleaming silver cups testified to the excellence of another product of Orange Hill—race horses, bred as a hobby by Mr. Barnard.

The air of comfort and peace that pervaded the house might have taken its tempo from the groves outside, for the production of coconuts cannot be hurried. As we relaxed before lunch, Mr. Barnard told me

49

Cloud-scraper volcano, 4,048-foot Soufrière cups a lake on St. Vincent. It last erupted in 1902,

that a palm does not bear until its eighth year, but that it lives to a venerable 70.

We began our meal with soup made from produce from the garden behind the house. We continued with fish that had been swimming off the beach the night before, went on to an estate-grown chicken, and ended with—coconut pudding!

French wines accompanied the meal, but also on the table was a chilled carafe from which another glass was filled. "All my life I have drunk coconut water instead of rain or well water," our host explained. "Now I find that every other kind tastes flat." Sipping my own and finding it faintly fragrant but not sweet, I could agree.

Before we left Orange Hill Mr. Barnard showed us mute testimony to the horror of the 1902 eruptions of Soufrière, when 2,000 people perished. He pointed out a squat stone building near the copra-drying

blanketing the area with ash as black as coal dust.

ovens. "Underneath is a cellar where rum was stored when the plantation grew sugar cane. It has only one door and one small window, which can be tightly closed.

"When flames began to shoot from the crater, and a black cloud rolled down the mountainside, 40 people working nearby crowded into this cellar. They were the only survivors on the estate. The manager and his wife, who were Scots, were among them, but couldn't stand the heat and smell. They left and ran towards their house. Two days later they were found dead on the steps, victims of the cloud's superheated steam and a lack of oxygen."

Soufrière's heat charred trees and plants at Orange Hill. It blighted crops, roasted cattle where they fell, and even overpowered birds on the wing. On the slopes to the north the lands once deeded to the Caribs suffered even more, but most of the Indians were spared. Because of a revolt many years before, practically all of them had been banished to the island of Roatán off Honduras.

One benefit stemmed from Soufrière's eruptions. Dust from the towering clouds has enriched the soil not only of St. Vincent, but also of Barbados, 100 miles to windward where air currents carried the fallout. So heavily did the "May Dust" fall there after an eruption in 1812 that day turned into night, causing some Barbadians to think the end of the world had come.

After my trips to the interior, Kingstown seemed a busy seafaring center. Since my last visit, modern docks had been built, so that produce no longer has to be carried into the water on the heads of stevedores, and then rowed in clumsy lighters to freighters waiting offshore.

But not all is modernity. I found a bulletin board announcing the departure of vessels in the language of the past when schedules were dictated by the vagaries of wind and tide and the availability of cargo. "Notice," I read in bold, crude lettering. "The auxiliary schooner *Alwood* leaves for

Aboard the tender, Davis communicates by walkie-talkie with skipper Mitchell on *Finisterre*. The fiber-glass Boston Whaler taxied the crew from ship to shore, towed water-skiers, and poked among reefs. From the craft, NATIONAL GEOGRAPHIC photographer Winfield Parks made pictures of the yawl.

51

Grenada on or about Tuesday 19th January taking passengers and cargo." Below, less prominently scrawled: "God willing."

The universal meeting place of yachtsmen and cruise-ship visitors ashore was the Beachcomber, a small cafe near the waterfront. Its bamboo walls are decorated with sea fans and shells; a large rack holds well-thumbed magazines from England and the United States, some of venerable vintage; tables spill out into a garden; and waiters never hurry leisurely clients.

As I relaxed one day at a corner table, proprietor Alan Gibbings told me how the Beachcomber came about. "Many years ago I was living in India. I read your account of *Carib*'s cruise in the NATIONAL GEOGRAPHIC and decided to visit the West Indies. I settled in St. Vincent and look—the result!"

IN CONTRAST to the pleasures of the Beachcomber, the roadstead of Kingstown gave me some of my worst moments of the winter. Henry Davis reported that both of *Finisterre*'s 45-gallon water tanks were getting low, so we arranged through Kenneth Punnett to go alongside the town wharf, where the fire brigade would connect a hose.

Unfortunately, the same heavy surge that greeted us on our arrival from the Grenadines was still running, and the undulations became steeper as they neared shore. Only on going alongside did I realize the power in the lazy surges. Heavy cork-filled fenders protecting *Finisterre*'s fragile wooden topsides from the concrete quay were flattened, and our lines seemed to shrink to half their diameter as each lunging crest passed under. Should anything break under the strain, serious damage could result.

Yet comedy soon mixed in. A fireman in full uniform standing on the wharf saluted and ambled away, when seconds counted. After long moments he returned with two helpers, dragging a firehose complete with polished brass nozzle. On being told nothing else was available, I passed it below to Henry as fast as I could.

The chief fireman sauntered to a distant valve and loosed a surge of water; the flat ribbon fattened into a plunging python. My fight to keep *Finisterre* from crashing into the wharf was nothing to the battle which began below. Shouts rose through the companionway, punctuated by a mighty splashing as Henry struggled to direct the jet into the small tank openings. Finally Henry, the hose, and a geyser of water catapulted to the deck. When the chief fireman finally turned off the stream, Henry looked into the cabin to discover that as much water had sprayed onto our bunks as into the tanks!

Our tribulations continued into the night. We rolled past Fort Charlotte into what should have been the calm lee side of the island. But the velocity of the trade winds and the resulting seas in the West Indies vary from year to year, and chance had brought us south during an unusually fresh cycle, accompanied by overcast skies and frequent rain squalls.

Now Soufrière's upper slopes were shrouded in cloud. Looking in at Buccament Valley, I could see the broad leaves of the banana plants flogging like sails, while white foam streaked the normally placid water near the beach.

Off the town of Chateaubelair the roadstead was a little better. Win Parks and Ken Punnett, having come by car, waited for us on the wharf. Going ashore in the Whaler, I found that in one respect the village had not changed—the local bathing-suit salesmen still made little profit on the junior boys' sizes. Children romped in the shallows and played hide-and-seek among fishing canoes. A single street ran between cottages dwarfed by breadfruit trees and coconut palms. We stopped in a little shop to treat ourselves to a lump of that rarity of the tropics, ice; then we returned to *Finisterre* in the Whaler.

As we climbed aboard, the sun dropped below a cloud to hang above the western Caribbean as a glowing disk. From it a magic carpet unrolled across the sea to our deck. Touched by the warm light, St. Vincent was transformed. In the village, hibiscus and poinsettia burst into flame. Beyond, green hills cast purple shadows into valleys, like a velvet robe swirling upward to meet Soufrière's glowing crown of cloud. It is in such moments that the traveler of the byways is rewarded for the discomforts.

Below palm-tufted heights of Chateaubelair Bay, *Finisterre* rests after a night of unexpected squalls and swells off St. Vincent. From this haven the author steered for St. Lucia's twin peaks.

IV St. Lucia: Island of Green Gold

Glistening banana boat awaits cargo in St. Lucia's Port Castries, the sea-flooded crater of an ancient

IN THE MORNING, as we cleared Chateaubelair Bay, my first order to the helmsman was, "Steer for the twin peaks." As usual in the southern islands, navigation was simple. Leaving one island, we always had the next in sight, and for almost three hundred miles we needed no compass.

This time we had a special target. The golden light of dawn clearly silhouetted the Pitons of St. Lucia, for me a unique landfall even after having seen much of the world from the deck of a small boat. Like Grenada and St. Vincent, St. Lucia is of volcanic origin, with a central spine of wooded mountains falling away on all sides to the sea. But on the southwestern corner of St. Lucia the pattern is broken by two mighty outcroppings, conical peaks standing as sentinels visible from afar.

As we drove across the channel under reefed sails, the spires became ever more impressive. To port, Petit Piton towered 2,461 feet, rising almost vertically from the Caribbean, while to starboard Gros Piton lifted even higher but not so steeply. With the awe of entering a cathedral, we crept into the bay between.

Continuing along the western coast, we arrived off Marigot Harbour at dusk. In this lovely sailor's retreat, a deep, narrow

volcano. *"Statio Haud Malefida Carinis"* — "A Reliable Shelter For Ships" — proclaims the island's motto.

TED SPIEGEL, RAPHO GUILLUMETTE

inlet between high hills, a palm-grown sandspit forms a barrier against the sea. Beyond the spit, we dropped anchor in flat water that reflected stars. For the first time since leaving St. George's *Finisterre* had no movement on deck or below.

With the morning I found changes in Marigot Harbour. A small hotel had been built on one shore, a row of rental cottages on another, while a real estate development impended. Even so, I was hardly prepared for the full extent of the boom.

George Eggleston, an American writer who owns properties near the bay and the capital city of Castries, told me: "In the twenties and thirties, before modern tourism, the government was anxious to dispose of uncultivated land to settlers. They asked from 10 to 20 shillings an acre—about $2.50 to $5.00 then. Even when you were here in *Carib* you could probably have bought all the land surrounding Marigot Harbour for $1,500. Now one small area has been subdivided into 226 one-third-acre lots at an average price of $5,000—which adds up to $1,130,000!"

Castries had altered also. Missing were the weathered red roofs and pastel houses of the other islands. Where before we had lain at anchor in the busy port and rowed ashore for supplies, I now docked at a modern yacht facility, complete with laundry, frozen food, restaurant, and showers.

I was not long in finding the reason for the change in Castries. Standing on the terrace of Government House, I commented to the Administrator, Capt. Gerald Bryan, C.M.G., O.B.E., M.C., that the city had changed more since my cruise of 1947 than any I had yet visited.

"A disastrous fire swept Castries on the night of June 19, the year after you were here," Captain Bryan said. "Four-fifths of the town was destroyed. It started in a tailor's shop, and strong winds fanned the flames out of control. The entire commercial section and many government buildings were lost. The library was gutted, as were the banks, the cable and wireless office, and the newspaper plant. Then there was a second fire in 1951, not quite so

Chartered yachts stand motionless in sun-polished Marigot Harbour, south of Castries. Swinging outward from a palm-shaded beach, a tender returns visitors after a trip ashore.

Nearing the Pitons of St. Lucia, *Finisterre* beats to

NATIONAL GEOGRAPHIC PHOTOGRAPHER WINFIELD PARKS (ABOVE) AND TED SPIEGEL, RAPHO GUILLUMETTE

windward. Davis, "a fellow veteran of midnight battles with flogging sails," tightens the genoa's leech-line.

serious, but more dwellings were destroyed while housing was still a problem."

Since rebuilding, Castries looks more like a town in Florida than one in the Windward Islands. Glass-fronted department stores replace dim shops, the banks and other buildings are completely modern, and there is an air of bustle in the business district. In fact, on getting a much-needed haircut, I found that at least one businessman operates in two spheres at the same time.

As I took my place in the usual chair facing the traditional row of colored bottles of scalp tonic, I saw in the mirror that the other half of the barbershop was a photographic studio, complete with a camera on a tripod and a painted backdrop. "I'm sorry I can't give you a shampoo," said Mauricette, the proprietor, "but I'm washing prints in the sink."

Yet on pushing beyond the streets of

57

Banana "headers" at Port Castries load plastic-wrapped stems of fruit into the hold of a refrigerated ship that will carry the cargo to Britain. Islander with a gasoline-powered blower (left) sprays the "green gold" trees against leaf spot.

Castries I found St. Lucia still based on a plantation economy, and the rugged section near the Pitons as remote from the 20th century as one of the lesser Grenadines.

One automobile expedition took Win and me around the island's southern section, beginning with a climb up Morne Fortune past the gate of Government House, and a descent into the valley behind to follow a coastal road. To our left was a green sea of bananas, for St. Lucia produces even more stems than St. Vincent; to our right was the blue of the Caribbean.

As the road snaked around the hillsides we could glimpse the Pitons, and finally we came to the village of Soufrière, snuggled under the shoulder of Petit Piton. There fishermen hauled nets into narrow dugout canoes as children splashed in the shallows; in the foreground roamed pigs, goats, and sheep. Beyond, climbing again, the road entered a rain forest of towering bamboo and giant fern, then abruptly came to a volcanically blighted area where not even a blade of grass could exist.

It was easy to see why these volcanic isles had their Soufrières (from the French *soufre,* meaning "sulphur"). Here the mighty natural forces which had lifted these peaks above the sea were still at work. Over witches' caldrons of black water and mud hung a mist pungent with the rotten-egg smell of sulphur. We picked our way along crater rims, which grew hotter as the slope rose, until finally we stood staring at a pit of bubbling yellow, barely visible through swirling clouds of reeking steam.

Nearby were springs whose curative powers so impressed a French governor in 1784 that he sent a sample of water to Paris to be analyzed by the doctors of King Louis XVI. As a result of their report, the king had baths erected here for the use of his troops.

In the early years of colonization, mortality from tropical diseases was far greater than from Carib arrows or enemy bullets. Neither malaria nor yellow fever had been

TED SPIEGEL, RAPHO GUILLUMETTE

traced to the mosquito, and everywhere water was stored in open cisterns. While the baths of Soufrière effected no miraculous cures, they undoubtedly comforted poor soldiers suffering from skin irritations caused by heat and insects.

Continuing toward Vieux Fort, we had the feeling of entering a forest wilderness. We did not pass a person or a wayside hut for so long that I wondered whether I had mistaken the road. Finally I saw a woman walking with a stem of bananas balanced on her head. I asked directions and found she could speak no English.

On an island that has belonged to Great Britain for a century and a half, her only language was a patois—a mixture of a few Carib and African words with a French

Sugar-loaf landmarks, the Pitons thrust above the village of Soufrière on St. Lucia's southwest coast. The cores of lava loom as remnants of volcanoes diminished by centuries of erosion.

TED SPIEGEL, RAPHO GUILLUMETTE

Youthful St. Lucian mends a 400-foot seine trailing from poles that hoist it for drying. Beyond, Petit Piton bulks 2,461 feet high. Boatmen (right) lower a close-meshed net into a longboat before a day of fishing. St. Lucia's peaceful occupations veil a bitter past—five times in the possession of the French and five times taken by the British between 1760 and 1814.

base. When I repeated my question in French, we could talk haltingly—at least I gathered we were on the right road.

Vieux Fort had been the site of an American base during World War II, part of the "destroyer deal." Before the United States declared war, it had turned over 50 ships to the British in return for 99-year leases at strategic Caribbean locations.

From Vieux Fort the United States had kept aerial watch over Martinique and surrounding waters during the years the Vichy government of France collaborated with the Nazis. There were rumors that German submarines fueled and took on supplies in Marigot Harbour. In 1942, a U-boat torpedoed and sank a Canadian passenger steamer and a cargo vessel at the wharf in Port Castries, then surfaced in the harbor and calmly proceeded to sea.

In contrast to the steep western coast near the Pitons, we found a windward shore that held broad, sloping fields. Cows grazed beside the idle runways of Vieux Fort, and, beyond, our way lay through lowlands once planted in sugar cane. Then the road began to climb over spurs jutting from the central spine. The towns of Micoud and Dennery huddled in deep semiprotected coves, where Atlantic surf creamed almost to the doorsteps of the houses. Crossing the cool mountain roof, we finally looked down again into the port of Castries.

The following day I received an object lesson in the fertility of St. Lucia when I walked with Mr. Eggleston to the boundaries of his estate, commanding a view of the harbor. We came on a workman driving stakes into the ground to close a gap in a line of flowering trees. Next to rich green leaves and pale pink flowers, the poles looked sadly bare. "Don't worry," said George. "That is *Gliricidia*. You cut off a branch at a joint, sharpen the end, stick it

in the ground almost anywhere, and soon you have a lovely flowering tree, or a fence if you plant them in a row. Given a few months these sticks will look like the rest."

St. Lucia is many things, yet I always think first of its history, which epitomizes the story of the island chain. It began with the familiar theme of discovery by Columbus, who sighted the island on his fourth voyage in 1502. It continued with the English and French fighting each other and the Caribs, while other land-hungry Europeans lurked in the wings.

The possession of St. Lucia was especially disputed, as Cardinal Richelieu deeded it to a French West Indies trading company at about the time Charles I of England included it in a grant of the "Caribees Islands" to the Earl of Carlisle. These acts of generosity with real estate that neither owned did not stop an intrepid Netherlands company from landing and trading there.

But the Dutch did not stay. Perhaps they were smoked out in the same fashion as the early English settlers in 1638. The Caribs built fires of red pepper plants to windward, creating a primitive gas attack which the colonists could not endure.

Clutching dolls, youngsters wait with their mother (above) at Vigie Airport near Castries. Planes call here twice daily, providing a link with the other islands.

In look-alike skirts and blouses, girls stroll back to work at a Castries bank after a coffee break. The city of 35,000 conducts most of the island's business.

Children clap hands to the rhythm of a song spinning from a record at St. Joseph's Convent in Castries. Many youngsters speak patois at home and explore English for the first time at sessions like this.

65

So often did St. Lucia change hands that it is impossible to trace the pattern here. The struggle reached its climax in the latter part of the 18th century. On the heights and surrounding waters centered much of the drama bearing directly on the destiny of the thirteen colonies to the north in their War of Independence. Had not a large part of Britain's naval and military strength been pinned down on St. Lucia and neighboring islands, it could have been employed against the forces of George Washington, perhaps with decisive results.

Five times in the possession of the French after 1760, five times taken by the British, St. Lucia was a strategic island. Commanding the town of Castries is Morne Fortune, the most bitterly contested prize of all. On its plunging slopes men died in windrows in many battles, toiling upward through withering enemy fire.

The British 27th Regiment showed such exceptional bravery in storming the heights at the point of the bayonet on May 24, 1796, that the commander honored the regiment by flying its colors over the captured fortress for an hour before hoisting the British flag. The seesaw of attacker and defender went on until 1814, when the island was ceded to Britain for the last time.

Everywhere I was reminded of the duality of St. Lucia's past, but especially walking the ghost-ridden parade grounds of Morne Fortune. Ruined barracks and other buildings testified to the frequent change in masters. The French built of stone, the British of brick. There are buildings of each, and a few of both where the engineers of one completed a job begun by the other.

The blending of cultures is equally apparent in food and in place names. Gallic herbs and sauces enliven the simplest native dishes, and maps show Londonderry as a village in the hills behind Anse de la Rivière Dorée, while Pigeon Island lies across from Gros Islet.

Only one present-day activity broke the serenity of Morne Fortune. Passing a building that had been the noncommissioned officers' barracks of the 27th Regiment, I heard hammering. Entering, I found a small cooperative factory headed by Rick Cochran, a Canadian who told me that he was in the West Indies because he once slept in the open at 70 degrees below zero, and had been moving south ever since.

Three years before, the local government, to stimulate enterprise and provide employment, had lent Cochran the unused barracks to make furniture and fiber-glass

Heading homeward after a hunt for dolphin and kingfish, fishermen hope their boat lives up to its name. Local lore says the cleaverlike bow of their pirogue resembles the rams of Carib war canoes. Spray-lashed boatmen ride out a squall off St. Lucia's southern tip (right).

dinghies based on a mold brought from Malta. Now his greatest hope was an experiment with a structural panel to be used in low-cost housing.

"Bamboo grows almost everywhere down here—cheap, light, and strong," Rick said. "We are trying to produce a sandwich with a bamboo core and fiber-glass skins. Our biggest trouble is with tiny boring insects that live in the cane. Natives say the number depends on the cycle of the moon at harvesting, but we haven't found their operating schedule or a chemical means of eliminating them."

DESPITE such budding industries, St. Lucia remains a planter isle, and 80 percent of its foreign exchange comes from the export of its green gold. "Banana-ship day" is an event that extends to remote fastnesses, where thatch-roofed huts form roadside pickup stations. Geest Industries, Ltd., whose ships transport the crop to England, has a rule that no more than 36 hours can elapse between cutting a stem and loading it into a refrigerated cargo hold. Thus when a trim vessel warped alongside the Castries wharf and threw open the doors in her white topsides, lines of women formed in an adjoining warehouse to meet lines of trucks winding down the hillsides.

Soon a procession began that reminded me of worker ants hurrying to empty an oversize sugar bowl. As each woman stepped forward, two men swung a plastic-sheathed stem of bananas to the top of her head, where she balanced it on a small pad. Almost at a run the woman set off for the ship, passing another line returning for a load. At each cargo door, two stevedores swung the stems into the chilled hold.

"The women load 1,000 to 1,200 stems per door per hour, and we usually work four or five doors at a time," a Geest official shouted to me above the din. "Each woman receives three cents 'BeeWee' for every stem she delivers. Before finishing tonight these women will have carried on their heads 1,000 tons of bananas.

"This is the only place in the islands where ships are loaded like this. It goes back to the days when steamers burned coal and Castries was a great fueling port. Then the women carried coal aboard in baskets. It is hard work, but 'headers' can make more in a few hours than they could on a plantation in a week."

On our final Sunday we took a busman's holiday, a picnic sail to Pigeon Island. Coming out of Port Castries with His Honour the Administrator and Mrs. Bryan as guests, we found the wind dead on the nose, and fresh. The sea is no respecter of rank, and dollops of spray blew aft to soak all hands. But the sun was bright and the water warm, and Captain Bryan smiled his enjoyment from the wheel.

As *Finisterre* drove rail down across Gros Islet Bay, I had the same feeling of association with history that I experienced atop Morne Fortune. For long weeks in 1782 a British fleet had lain at anchor here, guns loaded and sails ready on the yards, while tough old Admiral Sir George Rodney kept careful watch, looking through his telescope toward Martinique. There, under the shelter of shore batteries in Fort Royal, now Fort de France, rival Admiral Comte de Grasse was preparing the French fleet for a rendezvous with a force of Spanish ships at Santo Domingo.

Then, at dawn on April 8, a swift picket vessel brought word that De Grasse had left Fort Royal. Rodney swooped down in pursuit, sailing northward to the Dominica Passage, where the fleets clashed in the Battle of the Saintes. After a fierce sea fight, De Grasse struck his colors, giving Britain supremacy in the West Indies. Soon we too would sail for Dominica, following in Rodney's wake.

Next day, clearing at the Customs House in Castries, I received a document unchanged in form and substance since Rodney's time, when every vessel mounted cannon for protection against pirates. "These are to certify to all whom it doth concern," ran the text, "that Carleton Mitchell, master and commander of the yawl *Finisterre*, burthen of 10 tons, mounted with 0 guns . . . and bound for Martinique, having on board ballast and broken stores, entered and declared his said vessel according to law." Armed with such formidable clearance, *Finisterre* stood boldly toward Martinique.

Reeking vapors swirl above pools of boiling mud and sulphur-laden water on Soufrière, St. Lucia's active volcano. The author steps cautiously toward the caldrons, his camera in hand.

V *Martinique:*
A Touch of France

Gleaming vision of Paris rises above the treetops on a misty hillside at Balata, north of Fort de France

A WILD RIDE began as we left the shelter of the land. Although the sun shone brilliantly, small black clouds drifted in from the open Atlantic. Each carried its own fresh packet of breeze, adding an extra zip to the already strong trades.

Clad in oilskins, I was at the wheel while Henry stood by the main halyard. Should we have to reduce sail, Henry could crank in a reef as I handled chores in the cockpit. Long practice together made it a comparatively simple operation. But, as always, we were reluctant to shorten down unless the wind left us no choice.

Now we were on the edge. In the lulls, *Finisterre* needed the power of all the sail she could carry to drive through the seas; otherwise she would plunge and be stopped by each successive crest. On the other hand, in the squalls she was buried, and wallowed rather than slicing ahead. The lee deck became a millrace of rushing spume, and even the liferail stanchions vanished. To ease the ship or carry on? I was faced with a dilemma as old as sail itself.

When we had nearly crossed the channel, an especially vicious puff forced us far down. Suddenly I had a moment of panic. Win Parks was not in sight—and a man overboard is a skipper's worst nightmare.

Martinique's church of Sacré Coeur echoes the style and name of the great basilica of Montmartre.

Instinctively I let *Finisterre* come up; there was Win, clinging to the lee main shrouds. He was completely buried during the plunges, yet operating a waterproof camera with an outthrust arm whenever he could see!

After such a rough crossing, we could appreciate one of the British Navy's great feats as we slammed past Diamond Rock, off the southwest corner of Martinique. In 1803, a British squadron had imposed a blockade on the French, but Commodore Sir Samuel Hood found supply ships slipping past in the narrow channel between Diamond Rock and Martinique.

To seal the gap, in January, 1804, Hood anchored his flagship *Centaur* as close to the Rock as he dared. A detachment of sailors climbed to the summit and fixed a tackle to a pinnacle. Laboriously they hoisted five cannon, reminding a witness of "mice, hauling a little sausage."

For 17 months, 120 men and boys held

H.M.S. *Diamond Rock* — in 1804, with Britain and France at war, the Rock southwest of Martinique became a bastion of the British fleet and a commissioned sloop of war. From its sheer heights, 120 sailors-turned-mountaineers cannonaded French ships running the blockade of Fort de France. In the contemporary engraving, defenders hoist provisions to the garrison on the Rock, still saluted by British Navy vessels.

Mountainous Martinique lies halfway between Dominica and St. Lucia. Its people speak Creole, a patois, and French, the official language.

the Rock under the command of Lt. J. W. Maurice and harassed enemy shipping. Not until June 2, 1805, was the brave band dislodged. A heavily armed French squadron consisting of two line-of-battle ships, a frigate, a corvette, a schooner, and eleven gunboats took the Rock at a loss to themselves of 30 killed, 40 wounded, and three gunboats destroyed, against two men killed and one wounded on the British side.

As we sailed close, Diamond Rock looked

NATIONAL GEOGRAPHIC PHOTOGRAPHER WINFIELD PARKS

like a great stone haystack, with almost vertical sides and a crown-shaped top. Seas boiled against the base and shot upward like geysers. Nowhere could we see a convenient place to land supplies, while a climb to the top seemed in the province of mountaineers, not sailors.

Proud of the pinnacle, the British commissioned it H.M.S. *Diamond Rock*, a sloop of war. And it appears that way today on Admiralty records. A supply ship attached to the garrison also took the honored name. Passing Royal Navy ships still fire a seven-gun salute as they pass the Rock, and *Finisterre* likewise dipped her colors in tribute to the bygone era of wooden ships—and iron sailormen.

Beyond, in Fort de France Bay, a magnificent body of blue water almost surrounded by rolling green hills, three cruise ships swung at anchor, and passengers shuttled to a landing near La Savane, a park in the center of the city. Following maritime procedure, we hoisted the yellow quarantine flag to signal that we wished to enter the waters of another sovereign country.

Funneling wind and marching whitecaps made me think longingly of an inner harbor, Le Carénage, remembered from *Carib*'s visit. So, when no boatload of officials came out, I committed a minor transgression and powered around Fort St. Louis to the millpond Carénage behind.

We were made welcome as soon as we warped the stern in to the quay near the yacht club. Mail forwarded in care of my friend André Garcin was delivered, and soon we were being driven toward La Savane in a car he had sent.

For 18 years André and I had corresponded. He is director of Crédit Martiniquais, the island's foremost bank, and an ardent yachtsman. We had seen each other only once in the interval, yet such is Martinique hospitality that all was arranged for our reception.

As the chauffeur whisked us from the secluded Carénage to the center of Fort de France, my eyes widened. I looked out at

Carnival revelers and parading floats throng Fort de France in a pageant lasting from mid-January until midnight on Ash Wednesday. The streets resound with the rhythm of the popular beguine, a dance that originated on Martinique.

75

boutiques displaying Dior neckties, Hermès scarves, and Chanel perfumes, much like a miniature of Rue St. Honoré, a chic shopping street of Paris. Gourmet food shops offered pâté de foie gras and fresh grapes flown from France.

In sidewalk cafes couples sipped apéritifs, or lone men sat hunched over a newspaper—*France-Antilles* instead of *France-Soir,* but the atmosphere was the same. Suddenly I felt I had made a great mistake in my navigation and somehow had sailed *Finisterre* from the West Indies to Europe.

Later, when I told André Garcin of my feeling, he smiled. "But you *are* in France, *mon ami.* Since March 19, 1946, Martinique has been a department of the Republic, with representatives in the Chamber of Deputies, and the rights and responsibilities of any other department.

"The only difference is the climate and the ocean between. We see films in the cinema at the same time, our young people dance to the same music, our wives wear the same hats and dresses."

Fort de France is often called "the Paris of the Antilles," but to me it is more like Marseille, with its busy waterfront and ship-repair yards, its mixed population and hot sunshine, its complex of industry set into a productive countryside. After the leisurely pace of the other Windwards, it was a shock to be part of bumper-to-bumper traffic jams, with gendarmes trying to hurry cars rather than slow them down.

Although Martinique lives very much in the present, I found many reminders of the past. The foremost is a memory of an island maiden, Marie Rose Joséphine Tascher de la Pagerie, who grew up to become Napoleon's empress and to preside over the most glittering court of Europe.

One of my favorite places to rest after rambles through the city was a bench in the park near a statue of Joséphine in her coronation robes. Surrounded by palms rustling in the warm wind, she gazes across the glittering waters of the bay toward her birthplace, the village of Les Trois Îlets.

Visitors to nearby Pagerie Plantation see a pool where she may have waded as a girl. Though little remains of the family estate and though the small museum there fails to evoke either her childhood or later life, Martinique has not forgotten Joséphine.

Most of the year La Savane park is a quiet

"My heart is free," signifies the single protruding point of the bright madras headdress of a costumed Martinican wearing Creole earrings.

Martiniquais in their embroidered blouses and traditional skirts dance for visitors aboard the French Line cruise ship *Flandre,* docked at Fort de France, capital of Martinique. Bargain-seekers (below) crowd the counter of a free-port store to shop for perfumes and cosmetics.

backwater, but during carnival season masked revelers make it a swirl of gaiety. "In Martinique the carnival is special," I was told by Mme Yvonne Calvert, a lady I had met on a previous visit. Long an associate of Groupe Folklorique Martiniquais, organized to preserve vanishing peasant dances, she knew all about local customs.

"Here carnival goes on for six weeks. Each Sunday there is a different theme for the maskers. One week it may be 'Martinique in her native dress,' when even little children wear the foulard and the pointed madras headdress. Another week we may have 'Pierrot and Pierrette' clown costumes.

"On other islands, Mardi Gras is the climax, the end of carnival. But here it goes on until midnight of Ash Wednesday, and the last day is unique. Everybody dresses in black-and-white costumes, mourning King Carnival, who is to die in a few hours. He is carried in effigy through the streets and burned at dusk in La Savane or on a barge anchored offshore. But the merrymaking goes on until midnight, with the crowds singing, '*Vaval pas quitté nous,*' 'Carnival don't leave us.'"

THE EXUBERANT SPIRIT of the Martiniquais finds expression in the beguine, a dance popularized throughout the world by Cole Porter. It shows, too, in the colorful dresses of the women.

At the turn of the century author Lafcadio Hearn described the people as "fantastic, astonishing—a population of the Arabian Nights." He was especially struck by the women's characteristic headdress,

Waxy anthuriums bloom in a rain-forest plantation near Fort de France. Mme Joseph Bonne, wife of the estate's owner, snips flowers for export to France and West Germany. Her son places them in vials of water before packing.

FRED WARD, BLACK STAR

"an immense Madras handkerchief, which is folded about the head with admirable art, like a turban;—one bright end . . . being left sticking up like a plume."

The madras headdresses are still often seen, but with an innovation since the day of Hearn. As many as four points are left protruding. Having heard conflicting stories about the meaning of the number of points, I asked Mme Calvert.

"One point signifies 'My heart is free—I'm looking for a friend,'" she replied. "Two points mean 'I am promised; you are wasting your time.' Three points, 'Don't bother me—I'm happily married.' But four points signal, 'I'm not exactly free, but there is room for one more in my life.'"

Martinique is one of the most popular stops on Caribbean winter cruises, and when crowds pour ashore every taxi on the island capable of wheezing up a hill converges on the boat landing. Streets fill with visitors wearing fresh red sunburns and weird straw hats, mementos of other ports.

The shops swirl with confusion, looking like cartoons of ladies at a bargain sale, for time is short and French perfumes and kindred items sell at free-port prices. Often among the final sidewalk purchases is a madras handkerchief, which a smiling local *vendeuse* ties into a headdress before *madame* goes back to the ship—usually with one or four points left sticking up. Win and I wondered if the good ladies knew what they were signaling in the island code!

79

In contrast to the gaiety of Fort de France, the former capital city of St. Pierre still lies under the pall of one of the great tragedies of the 20th century. On May 8, 1902, a cloud of incandescent gas and superheated steam burst from Mont Pelée to envelop the town at its base.

Lafcadio Hearn, in *Two Years in the French West Indies,* had called St. Pierre "the quaintest, queerest, and the prettiest withal, among West Indian cities." In seconds it was reduced to ruins. Except for one prisoner confined in a hillside cell, all the people in the city—some 30,000—perished.

At the museum of St. Pierre I met the curator, Joseph Bonnet-Durival, 74 years old, who told me about the eruption. Through his cataract-blinded eyes I had some vision of what the awesome moment might have been like.

"I was 11 years old and remember it well," he said as he tapped his way between display cases with a cane. "My father had moved us out of town, toward Le Carbet. I saw the cloud of steam coming down toward St. Pierre with a dreadful noise, carrying ashes and stone but no lava, moving with terrific speed.

"The ships in the harbor were overwhelmed and sunk, all except the *Roddam,*

PAINTING BY PAUL CALLE

One escaped: Of 30,000 people, only Ludger Sylbaris survived—in a thick-walled cell that held him in solitary confinement. Deep volcanic ash nearly buries the door.

May 8, 1902: Incandescent gas and superheated steam explode from Mont Pelée, blacking out the sun and turning the city and harbor of St. Pierre into a flaming caldron. "It was like witnessing the end of the world," said the captain of the steamer *Roddam,* only vessel in the harbor to stay afloat. Correspondents (right) explore ruins of Rue Victor Hugo, once the Broadway of a gracious French colonial city.

81

Dusk-veiled Mont Pelée broods above the rebuilt city of St. Pierre, now home to only 6,300 people. Joseph Bonnet-Durival (above), curator of the local museum, holds a bottle fused by heat from the volcano. Moved out of the threatened city by his father when he was a boy of 11, he recalls a "dreadful noise," heard hundreds of miles. Pelée erupted at 7:50 in the morning and within three minutes transformed the city into a desert of ash. The watch (below) ticked on for 14 minutes before Pelée stopped it.

which was torn from her anchors and crept to St. Lucia with the news."

M. Bonnet-Durival pointed to grim relics in the museum cases: nails fused into a blob, a bunch of keys welded into a mass, cinders that once were books or food, the poor box from a church with the coins run together. Later, walking the still-scarred streets, I felt the town contained memories that could never be erased, even by the shouts of children playing among the ruins.

As might have been expected in a bit of France, dining was a delight everywhere in Martinique. In small bistros we had our choice of continental delicacies — *escargots*, the snails beloved by Gallic gourmets;

NATIONAL GEOGRAPHIC PHOTOGRAPHER WINFIELD PARKS (ABOVE) AND FRED WARD, BLACK STAR

caneton à l'orange, duckling roasted with an orange sauce; and for dessert thin *crêpes Suzette* served in flaming liqueurs.

In waterfront restaurants we sampled dishes based on tropic ingredients unknown in the homeland, yet prepared with Gallic flair. Among these were *crabe farci,* crabs not of the sea but of the land, often found living in holes at the base of coconut palms. The crabs are fed for several days on pepper leaves as a purge and to improve the flavor; then the meat is picked out and baked in the shell.

Frequently the crabs were followed by "calalu," made from huge dark green leaves looking like giant spinach, a soup so rich and thick that it would hold a spoon upright. But my favorite dish was an exotic combination called *blaff:* fish boiled in a clear broth, served surrounded by dishes containing yams, breadfruit, ripe bananas, and *piment,* whole peppers — tiny but potent.

The eating technique is to mash a pepper into the broth, spoon it up with a morsel of fish, then put out the fire with a quick bite from one of the bland side dishes.

For a while the cosmopolitan aspects of Fort de France obscured the fact that Martinique is basically a planter isle. An invitation to lunch with my old friend Charles Clément at his Acajou Estate on the windward side put us back in perspective.

We drove through lush countryside to Le François, where fishermen sailed gommiers into the center of the town via a narrow canal that leads from the open Atlantic.

Housewives waited on the banks, ready to buy freshly caught *langoustes*, the clawless lobsters of warm waters. As each canoe landed, the fisherman balanced scales on the thwarts, but both he and the customer had to scramble to keep the potential dinner on the pans long enough to be weighed.

Acajou Estate was exactly as I remembered it, a 200-year-old mansion set on a terrace of faded-rose bricks, surrounded by giant trees. *Acajou* means "mahogany" in French, and the wide mahogany boards used in building the house have turned silver-gray with age. A jalousied porch surrounds a center room supported by beams —dark and cool, yet open to every stray breeze of summer.

O N A TABLE were ice, glasses, and ingredients of a Martinique punch, a subtle combination of white rum, sugar syrup, and lime. We were not yet to be introduced to it, however. Through a door bounded M. Clément, hand outstretched and eyes twinkling above a trim white beard. Like Acajou, he had not changed in the years of our acquaintance.

"Welcome!" he cried. "But before you enjoy an apéritif, come see what we are doing on the estate."

Unlike other planters we had visited, M. Clément had not only diversified his crops, but also had carried through to a finished product: He was one of the foremost producers of rum on the island. He showed us groves of bananas and fields of pineapples before coming to the most important staple, sugar cane.

Men and women swung long knives at the stalks, which they crammed into tractor-drawn wagons for transport to the factory at the foot of the hill. Iron rollers crushed the cane, and the juice ran through open sluices. After fermenting in huge vats, the juice was piped away for distillation, then aged in barrels.

"In colonial days, sugar cane was grown as widely among the islands as bananas are today," said M. Clément as we walked past clanking machinery and wheezing stills, "and almost every estate produced rum. But on the English islands they made rum as a by-product of sugar, first extracting molasses, which they distilled into alcohol. Here, we make rum directly from cane juice. In composition it is surprisingly like freshly pressed grape juice. Producing *rhum vieux*, our dark aged rum, is almost exactly the same process as making cognac."

After a luncheon of many courses, we sampled Rhum Clément which had slumbered in charred casks for 15 years, and the conversation turned to serious matters. M. Clément was vice-president of "V Plan," a five-year plan to increase production, industry, and tourism.

"Our greatest problem," he said, "is to combine mechanization with a rapidly expanding population. We must be efficient to reduce costs because by law we must pay the same salaries as in France, yet we must not only not cut down on jobs but also provide more. We seek ways to provide better housing, medical care, and schooling, but these things are made difficult by 9,000 more people each year."

During our last days, from well-stocked vintners I filled *Finisterre*'s cellar—the bilge under the cabin table—with the rich red wines of Bordeaux and Burgundy, the dry whites of Alsace, and the fruity rosés of Provence. Other shops yielded delights such as *grappe*, a creamy white cheese protected by a thick layer of grape seeds, *Camembert*, and blocks of *chèvre*.

Often on Martinique I encountered a courtesy described by earlier visitors: When I asked directions, a passer-by would accompany me to my destination, answering my thanks with a courteous bow and smiling, *"Pas de quoi, monsieur,"* before continuing on his way. This courtesy toward strangers even moved a gendarme to tear up a parking ticket when I showed him my U. S. driver's license. Thus our visit ended on a note of hospitality, as it had begun.

"Our nickname for Martinique is *'L'Île des Revenants,'*" said André Garcin in farewell, "which for us means 'the isle where people come back.' So we'll say *au revoir* and not goodbye."

In a rugged sea, *Finisterre* plows under squally skies, her main and mizzen framing the sail of a *gommier*. "She had been built for this, my dream ship: to carry sail and drive hard, to go anywhere in safety and in comfort," the author says.

VI Dominica: Nature's Wild Triumph

Fluted bases of the swamp bloodwood grope in the waters of a virgin forest on Dominica. Tangled

FROM A DISTANCE, Dominica seems timeless — mountains swathed in green, a mass of vegetation so luxuriant that nature is almost an enemy, an island where man's works are mere scratches. As *Finisterre* lifted to big rollers in the channel, I felt I might have been a Carib chief standing in the bow of a canoe, scanning the almost vertical shoreline, so little had it changed through the centuries.

Now we encountered some of our roughest sailing of the winter. The trades seemed to bounce off the mountains to double in force, while the seas became steeper. "We'll have to reef," I shouted to Henry as a torrent rushed over the lee deck and cabin trunk. Smoothly he cranked a generous roll of sail around the main boom, and I came back on course.

But even carrying a small jib, a smaller mizzen, and a drastically reduced mainsail, *Finisterre* was overpowered. Furious gusts snatched the crests from the seas and drove them into our faces with stinging force. Sail battens slatted like machine-gun fire as I luffed through a savage squall. "Down main!" I yelled, and for the first time in her career *Finisterre* was driven to minimum canvas. Primordial forces stalked the sea, to match the rugged terrain.

Even as *Finisterre* approached the capital city of Roseau, an end-of-the-world feeling

growth and pitching slopes give an eerie charm to this least-disturbed of the isles of the Caribbees.

HIBISCUS (ROSA SINENSIS),
APPROXIMATELY LIFE-SIZE

FALSE CHAMELEON, OR ANOLE
(AMEIVA FUSCATA), 2/3 LIFE-SIZE

Flora and fauna of a wild land: Dominica's dense rain forests shelter creatures as diverse as the tree-dwelling anole, its throat distended to woo or to warn, and the male Hercules beetle, whose awesome horns serve mainly in clumsy jousting with rivals. When the insect is airborne, seven-inch wings propel it at speeds approaching 50 miles an hour. Claws upraised, a freshwater crab (opposite) glares with periscope eyes, ready for a fight. The giant katydid crouches on a leaf, detecting sounds with sensitive organs in its front legs. A crimson corolla rings pollen-tufted stamens of the hibiscus (above). As many as forty of these radiant flowers blaze on a single bush.

FRED WARD, BLACK STAR

HERCULES BEETLE (DYNASTES HERCULES), LIFE-SIZE

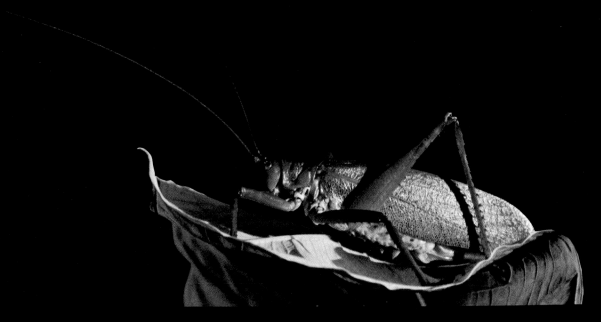

GIANT KATYDID (MASTOPHYLLUM SCABRICOLLE), LIFE-SIZE

FRESHWATER CRAB (GUINOTIA DENTATA), LIFE-SIZE

FRED WARD, BLACK STAR

persisted. There was no harbor, not even a bay. In every direction except east we looked upon the open Caribbean, while the chart showed soundings angling steeply to great depths. Attempting to anchor was somewhat like trying to hang on the sloping roof of a house.

Leaving Henry aboard with our heaviest anchor well set, Win Parks and I discovered that Dominica has a savage beauty all its own. It is the most primitive of the major islands. Lack of a harbor prevented growth of a port city, while the rugged interior discouraged the building of roads.

Not until 1956 were Roseau and Portsmouth, the two main cities, linked. Even so, the trip between the two is more than 50 road miles, although the actual distance is 20. Isolation is an old story for Dominica. The island was separated from friendly neighbors when the final diplomatic reshuffling left it an English colony lying between French Martinique and Guadeloupe.

Away from Roseau, I felt I was exploring a strange sea, a sea of lush vegetation. Waterfalls tumbled into wet green glades; giant bamboo and towering trees festooned with orchids arched above; and, tying all together, lianas strangled their hosts. Cultivated areas were hard to distinguish from the jungle. But occasional bunches of bananas or clusters of limes appeared through leafy frames.

I seemed engulfed in the sea of another planet, amid a confusion of hills and valleys as patternless as tide-ripped storm waves. As John Macpherson wrote in *Caribbean Lands, A Geography of the West Indies,* the island "is such a mass of peaks, ridges and ravines that in proportion to area it is more rugged than Switzerland."

Much of Dominica's character stems from the unusual rainfall. We were soon introduced to the phenomenon Dominicans call "liquid sunshine," a mist so fine that it can be seen only when back-lighted by the sun. Gently drifting from a cloudless sky, it gives a sensation more of coolness than of wetness. This is in addition to

Emerald Pool waterfall spills into a secluded forest glade draped with lianas and ferns. Stems of sun-flamed heliconia arch gently above a brook splashing among rocks toward the Belle Fille River, on the island's windward slope.

91

normal precipitation occurring in almost direct relation to the elevation.

"In sea-level Roseau we have an average rainfall of 75 to 80 inches a year," Gus Smith, one of the longtime residents, told me. "The Imperial Valley above the town gets about 130 inches. But as you move higher it increases, to more than 200 inches near Pont Cassé, 360 inches at Fresh Water Lake, and only the Lord knows what on the highest slopes of Morne Diablotin, which rises to 4,747 feet."

All of this contributes to the island's primitive quality. "Dominica is the least disturbed of the West Indian islands," a distinguished scientist told me in his field laboratory. Surrounding Dr. J. F. Gates Clarke, Senior Scientist of the Department of Entomology of the Smithsonian Institution, were massed specimens (including six-inch crickets) collected by the Bredin-Archbold-Smithsonian Biological Survey.

"The terrain is so steep, so wet, and so densely grown, it is difficult to exploit. This ties in with our objective: to study animal and plant life as it exists unaffected by civilization. Generally, when we leave the road we must hack our way every step with cutlasses. Tremendous tracts of untouched primeval forest remain here exactly as they were before the coming of Columbus."

Many years before, I had stayed with John Archbold at Springfield, a plantation high in the Imperial Valley, now a guesthouse as well as a producing estate. This time John was not in residence, but I called to find Millie, his housekeeper.

She served Win and me a memorable lunch as we sat on a terrace with the whole sweep of the valley beneath our feet. The first course was calalu soup. Then Millie brought on a steaming plate of what looked like fried chicken, but I knew from previous experience it was a creature that had never borne a feather.

In the forests of Dominica dwells a frog, called *crapaud* in its wild state, but "moun-

Imperial Road threads a rain-soaked crease in the island's hilly spine. The highway links the capital city of Roseau on the leeward coast with the airport at Melville Hall on the Atlantic side. *Leptodactylus fallax* (right) weighs 2 pounds, almost twice as much as a North American bullfrog. Islanders cook the forest creature they call *crapaud* and serve it as "mountain chicken."

tain chicken" when it appears on a plate as an island delicacy. Because of the rainfall and deeply scored valleys, Dominica has many rivers; residents say they number 365, "one for every day of the year." On their banks hunters capture the crapaud by night, when its eyes reflect torchlight. What Millie now offered us was a crapaud.

In taste and texture it surprisingly resembled chicken. But only after the platter was empty would Millie let us see what we had enjoyed. Then she brought in a live crapaud, a large frog with bulging eyes. "If I show them to folks first, they won't eat any," Millie explained.

The small colony of Europeans and North Americans on Dominica began under pioneer conditions. Bob Lord and Gus Smith hacked clearings out of the forest, and practically built homes with their own hands. Lord, a former automotive engineer, ended by making most of the furniture for his house.

William Bunting, born in Scotland but brought up on Beacon Hill in Boston, told me, "There are 17 Americans who are permanent residents and landowners. I moved here myself 16 years ago. If we didn't want to live at a slower pace we wouldn't have settled here.

"But we find it funny, the ideas some people have about Dominica. For years I was an amateur radio operator, and talked to fellow hams in the States. I finally got so I would say, 'Come on down; we no longer have rings in our noses, and haven't eaten a missionary in years.' "

Although this was said in jest, part of the

Dominica legend stems from the once-cannibalistic Caribs still living on the island.

The making of a Carib warrior began at birth. "As soon as a male child was brought into the world," wrote Jamaican Bryan Edwards in his history of the West Indies, published in 1793, "he was sprinkled with some drops of his father's blood.... The father... believing, that the same degree of courage which he had himself displayed was by these means transmitted to his son.

"One method of making their boys skillful, even in infancy, in the exercise of the bow, was to suspend their food on the branch of a tree, compelling the hardy urchins to pierce it with their arrows, before they could obtain permission to eat.... The Charaibes instructed their youth, at the same time, in lessons of patience and fortitude; they endeavoured to inspire them with courage in war, and a contempt of danger and death."

ALTHOUGH not quite so tall as most Europeans of the era, the Caribs were a strong and muscular people. They painted their faces and bodies crimson and disfigured their cheeks "with deep incisions and hideous scars, which they stained with black, and they painted white and black circles round their eyes," wrote Edwards.

"Some of them perforated the cartilage that divides the nostrils, and inserted the bone of some fish, a parrots feather, or a fragment of tortoise-shell... and they strung together the teeth of... enemies... slain in battle, and wore them on their legs and arms, as trophies of successful cruelty."

Yet to me there was another side of the coin. The Caribs considered all strangers as enemies, but "among themselves they were peaceable, and towards each other faithful, friendly and affectionate."

A priest-historian who sailed through the islands at the end of the 17th century, Jean Baptiste Labat, declared in a work quoted by Edwards: "There is not a nation on earth more jealous of their independency than the Charaibes.

"They are impatient under the least infringement of it; and when, at any time, they are witnesses to the respect and deference which the natives of Europe observe towards their superiors, they despise us as abject slaves; wondering how any man can be so base as to crouch before his equal."

Fishing pirogue takes shape under artful hands. An adz-hollowed *gommier* trunk forms the shell of the dugout; upper planking adds freeboard. Dominicans fell the trees at the time of the new moon — to prevent rot, they say. Similar to pirogues fashioned on St. Lucia and Martinique, the craft recalls the *kanaua* that bore Carib warriors. Oarsman and paddler (below) abet a hint of wind on their flour-sack mainsail, sprit-rigged for a twilight fishing run.

Many contemporary accounts relate that almost invariably the Caribs preferred death to surrender. But if some were taken alive, "the miserable captives commonly sunk under a sense of their misfortune, and finding resistance and escape hopeless, sought refuge in death from the calamities of their condition," according to an old translation of the French explorer Rochefort. If there were no other way out, a Carib kidnaped into slavery swallowed earth until he — or she, for the women were almost as fiercely independent as the men — died.

The rugged terrain and dense forests of Dominica were particularly suited to their style of warfare. The Caribs were well entrenched in their mountain stronghold. In spite of the Treaty of Aix-la-Chapelle of 1748, which reaffirmed that Dominica belonged to the Caribs, first the French and later the British violated its terms.

The British gradually managed to pin the Indians against a wild stretch of windward coast that now forms part of the Carib reservation. Established in 1903, the reservation's 3,700 acres extend about eight miles along the Atlantic.

Win and I began planning an expedition to visit the Caribs from the moment we stepped ashore. Through Gus Smith we met Alford Benoit, who owns a Land-Rover and is familiar with the way to the reservation, since from time to time he takes a government nurse in to care for the sick. Leaving Roseau, we followed Dominica's single hard-surfaced road.

We climbed over a spur of Morne Trois Pitons, then dropped down in a series of hairpin curves. Suddenly, as I glimpsed the sea, Alford abruptly swung the Land-Rover onto a trail hacked through the forest.

I held on tight as we forded a wide river, rattled over a swamp on a corduroy road of tree trunks, then ground up a rutted trail of slippery wet clay. Entwistle Rock loomed over us like a watchtower above the trees. "We're lucky," Alford grunted as he shifted gears. "No rain today. After a downpour, you can't make it."

My first glimpse of a Carib was of a girl, no more than five years old. Clutching a bottle filled from a stream, she stopped as we paused alongside. Her long hair was as black and smooth as Chinese lacquer, and her coppery features had a definite Mongolian cast.

She smiled and spoke to Alford in patois before trudging toward a small frame house above the road. "The women and children are less shy now," Alford said. "A few years ago they ran into the bushes and hid whenever a stranger appeared."

Not far beyond we came on a woman washing her family's clothes in a pool under a small waterfall. When she looked up, I was startled by her appearance: I had not really expected to find pure types, but rather "Black Caribs," descendants of runaway Negro slaves and Indians. But here I saw slanting eyes, high cheek bones, straight hair, and parchment-yellow skin. To me, it was a scene from the Far East. She might have been Korean or Vietnamese.

Continuing along the road, we came to a spectacular clearing. Long Atlantic rollers thundered against a rocky cliff and offshore rocks spouted like surfacing whales. Trees on the slopes surrounding a natural amphitheater formed a frame for a small church.

Palms swayed overhead, and flowers massed at the door of a tiny cottage.

At the sound of our engine, a priest came out to welcome us. Father Martin belonged to the French order of the Sons of Mary Immaculate. He had lived and worked among the Caribs for three years. A small, wiry, dedicated man, he had a sympathy and an understanding that affected everyone with whom he came in contact, even the simplest of his charges.

As we lunched in the rectory, we learned something of Father Martin's parishioners. "Here no one has any concept of time or distance. The only measurement is how long it takes to walk somewhere. Naturally, this is hazy, especially during the rainy season when walking is really a problem—on our clay paths you take one step forward and slip two steps back. Yet the children walk to school from Gaulette River, which takes an hour even in good weather, and people coming to church from distant settlements need twice that."

NATIONAL GEOGRAPHIC PHOTOGRAPHER WINFIELD PARKS

Descendants of conquerors: Only a few hundred "pure" Caribs remain of the thousands of man-eating Indians who burst from Brazilian jungles centuries ago to sweep the Lesser Antilles. Today they live on a reservation that stood as their forebears' last stronghold on Dominica. Chatting with the author, Chief Germandois Francis holds a crown-capped mace. Above, a Carib scrubs clothes in a creek. The features of the Indian below suggest Asian ancestry.

The church, erected in 1880, was blown down by hurricanes in 1916 and 1928. Though the Indians devotedly rebuilt it each time, they also cling to their ancient legends. "I went to Entwistle Rock with the chief to look for a grotto where the old Caribs practiced their own religion," Father Martin said.

"Our guide claimed his father had shown him the opening to the cave, but he couldn't find it; perhaps it had been blocked by a rockslide. In any case, the Caribs believe nobody can go in because it is guarded by a huge snake called *tête-chien*, meaning 'dog's head' in patois. The snake would eat any intruder before he could get out. The legend also says the grotto connects with the sea, because during storms many *touloulou*, a type of sea crab, are found on the slopes of Entwistle Rock."

After lunch, we walked deeper into the reserve to visit the chief. With the wild ocean as a backdrop, a partially finished dugout canoe hauled up on the beach, and Carib faces peering at me from behind boulders and trees, I felt farther than ever from the modern world.

The house of Chief Germandois Francis stood in the center of a clearing worn bare by shuffling feet. It was built of hand-hewn breadfruit planks, a structure not more than 10 feet wide and 15 feet long, divided into two rooms. Ceremoniously we were invited into the first, decorated by magazine pictures pasted on the wall. Among them the British royal family were prominent. Soon the 32-year-old chief came from the inner room, wearing a sash draped across the shoulder of his best suit, and carrying a silver-headed mace.

"That's a new mace," whispered Alford Benoit as other Indians arrived to gather

Enduring centerpiece in a windswept setting, the Caribs' Catholic church stands above a deso-late stretch of Atlantic coast. The parishioners' fierce ancestors once slew early missionaries.

around the chief. "The people look docile, but as recently as 1930 they flared up in what we call the 'Carib War' over smuggling of tobacco and rum. The Indians threw rocks at the police and armed themselves with sticks, so the police used guns. Two Caribs were killed, and two others seriously wounded. When police reinforcements arrived, Caribs drove them off.

"The rebellion was finally put down by the arrival of a Navy warship, H.M.S. *Delhi*, which fired star shells over the reserve and landed marines," Alford continued. "As a punishment, the kingship was abolished, leaving only the title of chief, and the royal mace was confiscated."

As we walked back toward the church, I asked Father Martin how many pure Caribs remained on the island. " 'Pure'?" he repeated. "It depends on what you mean by the word. Many are obviously of mixed blood. Few genealogical records exist, of course, but if you go on appearance—Mongolian features, straight black hair, slanted eyes, yellowish skin—about 400 Caribs survive. Their racial characteristics are extraordinarily strong.

"Many are types so like the Asian that after a visit last year by a Japanese nurse, I was besieged by questions from the Caribs themselves: 'Father, who was that pretty Carib girl? She never lived here. Where she come from?' "

Before we left, Father Martin said with compassion, "The great needs of the Caribs are education and opportunity. They make and sell baskets and dugout canoes, but there is no market on the reservation for what they grow. Would you like to carry bananas on your head over these steep trails, hoping to get them to Roseau?"

Although a better access road is under construction, questions are now being raised in the island legislature about the legality of the reserve's establishment in 1903. Other Dominicans are trying to settle on sections of land long considered the Indians'. Searches of records reveal treaties with past chieftains, but no clearly defined grant of land in perpetuity by the Crown.

The Caribs, faced with the possibility that their reserve really does not belong to them, have reached a vital crossroads: Loss of their land could mean loss of tribal identity itself—the final blow for this remnant of a once mighty people.

Back aboard *Finisterre*, we hove in the anchor and got under way with a rush as the bow swung off to a white squall funneling down the mountainside. When the squall passed, we resumed our usual leisurely leeward-calm progress, but felt more dwarfed than usual by the precipitous heights towering above.

We tipped our heads to stare up at the lower slopes of Morne Diablotin, impressive enough even though the peak was swathed in cloud. "The highest mountains are usually obscured by clouds," the *Sailing Directions* note.

But suddenly a caprice of the wind rent the misty veil. Like a moving spotlight the sun shafted across ridges and valleys, and then for a few minutes the whole mighty shape was visible, twisted into fantastic forms by violent convulsions of nature. The rain forests accented rather than softened the effect, so impenetrable that their tree trunks had never known sunlight or the passage of man.

Thus my final impression of Dominica reinforced my first: It is the most lonely and savage of all the Caribbee Isles.

Great pluming thickets wreathe bluffs along the windward coast of Dominica. Ceaseless pummeling by wind and ocean spray shaped the tangle of shrubs. The parrot *Amazona arausiaca* (left) perches in a lofty mountain haunt.

VII *Guadeloupe: Where Admirals Fought*

In a shadow-dappled sea, the Îles des Saintes guard the southern approaches to Guadeloupe. These

*B*EFORE OUR ANCHOR touched bottom off Bourg des Saintes, on Terre de Haut, one of the Îles des Saintes, I sensed a change. I remembered this little dependency of Guadeloupe as a scattering of neat small dwellings with faded roofs almost hidden by palms, and, below, a crescent of beach unbroken except by fishing boats. Now I gazed at a cluster of modern villas reminiscent of those along the Mediterranean Riviera.

On going ashore to clear *Finisterre*, I found the reason. "We now have *le tourisme*," said the wife of the gendarme.

For the first time since *Finisterre*'s cruise began, I felt I walked a street as a stranger. In the center of Bourg des Saintes, a small square I did not remember was laid out with concrete walks and benches, a single flowering shrub relieving its barrenness. Climbing to the crucifix overlooking the harbor—placed there to protect the fishermen who venture forth in narrow boats fitted with huge sails—I found that even it had changed. A garish string of colored electric light bulbs had been draped across the monument.

Yet nothing could change the magnificence of the water surrounding the tiny archipelago. The deep blue of the Dominica Passage, a channel with a history, separates Dominica and Guadeloupe.

As Columbus sailed through on Sunday, November 3, 1493, on his second voyage,

ranquil waters once swarmed with European warships contending for control of the Caribbean.

A trick of the wind and bold tactics gave victory to Admiral Sir George Rodney (above) in the decisive Battle of the Saintes in 1782. As British and French fleets exchanged broadsides, shifting wind disorganized the line of French ships, commanded by Admiral Comte de Grasse (be-

low). Rodney's ships drove through the gaps to cannonade the enemy from both sides. The crippled French fleet forfeited its admiral and his huge 110-gun flagship *Ville de Paris* (right) to H.M.S. *Barfleur.* Rodney's triumph firmly established British power in the Caribbean.

he bestowed names showing what was in his mind and heart: *Sancta Dominica,* because of its discovery on the Sabbath; *Sancta María la Gallante,* in honor of his flagship; *Todos los Santos,* for All Saints' Day, recently observed; and *Santa María de Gadalupe,* in gratitude to the Virgin's shrine he had visited in Spain to pray for the success of his voyage. As we sailed toward Guadeloupe these same islands were visible, bearing modern versions of the same names.

Here Admiral Rodney had caught up with the French fleet, a pursuit we had been retracing since leaving Gros Islet Bay on St. Lucia. The Battle of the Saintes is often cited as the turning point in West Indian history. Admiral Comte de Grasse had tried to avoid conflict after leaving Fort Royal to rendezvous with a Spanish squadron, which would have given the enemies of Britain a substantial advantage of ships and troops. But when one of his ships was

damaged in a collision, and in danger of being captured, De Grasse turned back and lost the opportunity to escape.

The two fleets moved in parallel lines but sailed in opposite directions, I told Win and Henry from the wheel while we lounged in the cockpit. The breeze was light and the Dominica Passage calm, just as it had been for the battle.

When the wind shifted, causing a gap in the column of French ships, Rodney seized the opportunity and cut through the enemy line. Five British ships followed and a sixth broke through at another point, dividing the French and bringing them under fire from both sides. It was the first time in a hundred years that the maneuver had been employed.

The French were thrown into disorder. They fought bravely but hopelessly. When De Grasse struck his colors, some 400 of the 1,300 men on his flagship were dead.

Guadeloupe's "split personality" offers volcanic heights on the west and coral-based lowlands on the east. Bisected by a channel, this department of France is home to 300,000 people.

The victory precluded any serious challenge to British sea power in the Caribbean.

Lazily we closed the shore of Guadeloupe, which is not one island, but two, looking on the chart like a lopsided butterfly, with the Rivière Salée cutting through the middle. The western wing, called Basse Terre, dips into the Caribbean; the eastern

103

Gay carnival madness erupts in Guadeloupe in early January, reaching a frenzy at Shrovetide. Calypso-singing revelers frolic in the streets through Ash Wednesday, when they reluctantly end their lively masquerade by "burying" carnival. Then the quiet Lenten period begins.

wing, Grande Terre, juts into the Atlantic.

Between the two wings a bay leads to the principal port, Pointe-à-Pitre, and as we neared it we became part of a bustling parade of island traders and ocean freighters. At the yacht club dock, *Finisterre* lay dwarfed by cargo ships, as trucks and buses rumbled along a street just astern.

"We build for the future," said Umberto Petrelluzzi, to whom I had a letter of introduction. His father, Leopoldo, had arrived from Naples about 1900 as the captain of his father's ship. The large, dynamic family is now part of the warp and woof of the cosmopolitan community. Guadeloupe long ago became a melting pot of peoples and cultures. In 1654, a Dutch sailor, "Pieters," landed at the site of Pointe-à-Pitre to give it his name.

When Umberto was too busy to show us around, he placed us under the guidance of a married daughter, Marily Gouyé. Everywhere in Pointe-à-Pitre we found bulldozers at work—tearing up streets, moving houses, scraping away hillsides. Tall new apartment houses gleamed in the sun, and a new industrial zone, with modern docks, was rising beyond the present port.

Presently we came to a community of small wooden houses laid out in string-straight streets ending at the seashore. "This community is officially named Lauricisque," Marily said, "but everybody calls it '*Citée Transit*,' because people live here on their way from one place to another. These houses, the best of the old slum dwellings, have been moved from the condemned areas to make way for new buildings. While here, waiting for new homes to be built for them, the people become acquainted with modern things they never had before."

I entered a small shop. An electric light shone over the counter, illuminating canned goods and soft drinks on the shelves, and a polished brass spigot gleamed over a basin in the corner. "Before, I had only candles or an oil lamp," explained the proprietor, "and I carried water in buckets. Here, we now have schools for the children, and the old folks are learning, too."

As Marily drove us farther afield, I felt that nature made Guadeloupe a transitional point in our winter's cruise. Rugged Basse Terre is like the islands we had visited to the south, a spine of mountains falling away to the sea, with bananas, coffee, and other crops of the lush uplands growing on its rain-soaked slopes.

Grande Terre is cast in the pattern of most of the Leeward Islands which lay ahead. Its low shores are fringed by beaches and reefs; its chief product is sugar cane —and, increasingly, tourists. At a hotel so modern in architecture that it reminded me of an airport terminal, bikini-clad girls bronzed around the rim of a free-form pool while water-skiers wove fanciful patterns on a shallow bay.

Like Martinique, Guadeloupe is an overseas department of France. It was fought over and changed hands during two centuries, in the wake of European politics. In 1794, during the Revolution in France, it repeated the Reign of Terror. A guillotine was erected in the placid square overlooking the harbor where *Finisterre* now lay. In all, 1,200 Royalists were executed.

The abolition of slavery in 1848 led to the recruitment of East Indians to work in the fields. One Sunday, driving with Marily

Gouyé, I saw how their descendants have their own customs, yet retain vestiges of Hinduism. Near the village of Capesterre we came on a blue-white-and-red pole topped by a flag bearing strange symbols.

"It is the temple of Changuy," said Marily. "I know the chief priest. If he gives permission, we may watch. But be careful not to go inside the sacred building with your shoes on." The temple was a low structure of unpainted concrete blocks, guarded by an image of Mandira, the warrior god, clad in red, a sword lying at his feet. Nearby, the chief priest stood beside a slim brown girl dressed in white. Her hair was unbound, falling almost to her waist, and her feet were bare.

"The family prays to find the girl a husband," whispered Marily after speaking to the priest. "She is past the usual age of marriage, and no one has asked for her hand."

As we watched, roosters and goats wearing garlands of flowers were brought before the girl. Each was blessed in turn and its head cut off with a single flashing sweep of a cane knife. Before each sacrifice the priest anointed the blade with lime juice and rum. Three drummers pounded a rhythm that gradually increased in tempo and volume. When the last animal lay kicking in the grass, the girl entered the temple behind the priest.

Almost hidden in clouds of incense, the statue of a goddess, Malieman, sat on a throne covered in pink satin. She had been fashioned from a department store mannequin, and through the open window I could see that she wore a bride's veil and carried a bridal bouquet. The girl stood before the goddess with bowed head as the priest chanted a prayer. Cymbals joined the throbbing drums and the incense became overpowering. The girl lifted her head to gaze at Malieman with shining eyes, and, suddenly, it seemed to me, she had become beautiful.

Leaving the temple, the girl walked with

NATIONAL GEOGRAPHIC PHOTOGRAPHER WALTER M. EDWARDS

Human hoist lifts wrapped bananas into a vessel at Basse Terre, administrative capital of Guadeloupe. Interisland ships (right) take on cargo at Pointe-à-Pitre. Nearby, in a community called *"Citée Transit,"* former slum dwellers adjust to modern homes while waiting for urban planners to rebuild their neighborhoods.

a springy step. The music became almost a triumphal march as the girl balanced on her head a wooden tray containing a bare cutlass and strode around the temple, followed by the priests and her family. Then the procession wound toward a nearby covered shed where I could see tables and cooking fires.

"They go to eat rice and a curry made from the sacrificial animals," Marily explained. "It will be a big lunch for all the friends and possible suitors. If the girl finds a husband, there will be an even bigger party after the wedding, in gratitude to the gods."

Although Pointe-à-Pitre is the commercial center of Guadeloupe, the administrative capital is Basse Terre, on the western side of the island of the same name. Wide avenues lead past impressive government buildings. Guadeloupe has as dependencies not only the nearby Saintes, La Désirade, Îles de la Petite Terre, and Marie Galante, but also more distant St. Barthélemy and the French half of St. Martin. In keeping with the island's dynamic spirit, extensive docks for loading bananas had been built since my visit in *Carib*.

Shops in Guadeloupe's capital city close at noon for a lunch hour likely to extend into *une petite sieste*, the Gallic equivalent of a Latin *siesta*. As Marily commented, "If you call at three o'clock the phone is answered in sleep."

A second town perches above Basse Terre. The tree-bordered streets of St. Claude are lined by the houses of affluent merchants and government officials who work at sea level but sleep on the cooler slopes. Yet we did not pause even there, despite a noticeable drop in temperature. The road climbed higher up the side of yet another volcano named Soufrière.

As our little car labored upward past toppled trees and sparse undergrowth, Marily told me, "Only about ten years ago it erupted smoke and ashes for two days, accompanied by two earthquakes. I was in school. We were in the chapel when the building began to shake. I saw a statue begin to sway, and a priest standing underneath stepped aside just as it fell."

Part of the desolation around Soufrière stems from the passage of Hurricane Cleo, which struck Guadeloupe a savage blow in 1964. According to Marily, practically all

Bounty from land and sea overflows in the market of Pointe-à-Pitre, Guadeloupe's economic center and largest city. Vendors entreat

customers in a patois of French colored with words borrowed from English, Spanish, and the Carib Indians. Along the modern docks, cargo ships unload Parisian clothing and perfumes. The local shops offer imported goods and island handicrafts at temptingly low prices.

Cautiously cleaving sluggish waters, *Finisterre* seeks the open sea via Rivière Salée. The channel leads to hazardous coral-fanged shallows requiring the skill of a local pilot. Mr. Mitchell preferred this hour-long short cut to the safer

NATIONAL GEOGRAPHIC PHOTOGRAPHER WINFIELD PARKS

day-long route around Guadeloupe. Before leaving the island, he treated his guests to a shipboard dinner of *langouste*, cheese, salad, and wine (left) and, like the sunbathers below, enjoyed the palm-canopied beach at Sainte Anne.

the bearing cacao and vanilla trees had been destroyed, along with most of the bananas. Cleo also wrecked 5,000 concrete-block houses and 15,000 wooden homes. In the words of historian Bryan Edwards, hurricanes remain "those dreadful visitations," despite improved warning services.

Marily told me to pull off the road, and we walked to a shaded grove where trees overhung a pool fed by a brook bubbling over moss-covered stones. The chill air evoked little enthusiasm when Marily suggested a swim. Through a leafy frame we looked down on the Saintes, and beyond could see the looming bulk of Dominica. Marily produced a luncheon hamper, and magically spread not only island delicacies on a cloth, but also two of the wines of France, a white and a red.

On the way back along the northern coast of Basse Terre, the road for a while paralleled a river bed. A small stream meandered among boulders to discharge into the Caribbean. From the looks of the banks, I saw that sometimes the water level must be higher, but I hardly envisioned the torrent described by Marily.

"Once during the hurricane season we were having exceptionally heavy rains. A man driving along this road heard a sound of roaring water, so he left his car and climbed to higher ground. He saw his automobile disappear, and made his way to town across the fields.

"When he came back three or four days later the river had receded, but his car was gone. The police could find no trace of it. Then, months later, a skin diver swimming along the shore saw something strange. He dove down and found the car—almost a quarter of a mile from where the owner had left it!" But Guadeloupe has many nooks untouched by the violence of nature. One afternoon at sunset Umberto Petrelluzzi took us to an island his father had bought many years before, and kept as a bird sanctuary.

Using the Whaler, within minutes we had skimmed out of Pointe-à-Pitre's inner harbor to Îlet à Petrelluzzi, in sight of unloading ships and the city skyline. It was so quiet I became aware of a strange sound as we stepped ashore, like hundreds of tiny castanets. I asked Umberto the source, and he listened for a moment, then smiled. "Ah! You hear the little clams on the flats!"

We walked paths bordered by tropical flowers and bamboo. Doves flew overhead and golden pheasants exploded from nearby thickets. "Counting native birds, migrants, and those we have introduced, we have had 59 varieties on the island," Umberto said. "Except for a few we pen while they are being acclimatized, the birds are free to come and go as they please. The only cage is the island."

As our departure time drew near, I studied charts. Going through Rivière Salée would save us a long detour around either of the wings of Guadeloupe, but we would need a pilot to guide us through the dangerous reefs of the Grand Cul de Sac Marin, to the north.

Our problem was solved by a young man named Jean Rey, whom I met at the yacht club. Small and bouncy, he seemed to have only one uniform ashore or afloat: scanty swimming trunks and large sun-glasses.

"La Rivière Salée? Know it? Not many boats go through, but I know it like zat!" he exclaimed, pointing to a crack in the table between us. And he went on to prove his nautical knowledge with businesslike questions about the height of *Finisterre*'s mast and depth of keel.

Like all visitors, I had been told that Rivière Salée is "the only stream in the West Indies flowing between the Atlantic Ocean and the Caribbean Sea." I'm not sure what I expected, but I found a tidal channel reminding me of the Florida Everglades.

Green water flowed sluggishly between tree- and rush-bordered banks, patterned by small islands where the roots of mangrove trees splayed like the legs of insects. As Rivière Salée led north-south instead of east-west, it seemed to me to connect the two culs-de-sac of Guadeloupe rather than two mighty ocean basins. But if Rivière Salée failed to live up to its billing, the reefs of Grand Cul de Sac Marin were real. Unmarked coral fangs lifted on both sides, most invisible until we were close abeam. Jean steered with a foot on the wheel, as casual as he had been at the yacht club.

Then we made a final S-turn, and just before sunset only a single reef lay ahead. Breakers curled high along its length and sent spume trailing downwind like smoke. It seemed a barrier no boat could pass, but Jean pointed to a channel in the center where the swells lifted but did not break.

"Steer through the gap and you can go to Iceland without hitting anything," he said jovially. In an hour and ten minutes we had cleared Guadeloupe, a passage which would have taken a full day had we gone around either of the wings.

Tucking the fee I paid him into his swimming trunks, Jean shook hands and dived overboard to swim to a motorboat that had followed us. Henry Davis paused in hoisting the mainsail to laugh. "That's what I really call 'dropping the pilot'!"

Big-boomed boats and coolie hats distinguish Saintes seamen. Introduced from the Orient, the hats are fashioned of bamboo and cotton.

Basse Terre's Soufrière (foreground) shares its name with other volcanoes scattered among the isles of the Caribbean. Dense, boggy moss hides the lava plug of the crater. On lower slopes grow liana-laced rain forests and giant ferns.

VIII Antigua: A Harbor's Storied Past

A key to British naval might in the Caribbean, English Harbour on Antigua provided a haven where warships refitted to avoid the long voyage across the Atlantic. A hilltop fort guards the entrance in this 19th-century aquatint.

WHEN THE SUN set behind the mountains of Guadeloupe's Basse Terre, a full moon lifted over Grande Terre. The palette of the tropic sky began with sweeping strokes of red and gold to the west, but slowly softened through shades of rose to the palest lavender. As the moon climbed and brightened, it transmuted the sea into molten silver.

A fresh breeze waited beyond Pointe de la Grand Vigie, driving us rail down on a course of north. But not wishing to cross the 40-mile channel until dawn lighted the way into Antigua's English Harbour, we lowered the mainsail to slow down.

Even so, we rushed through the night, with spray glittering as it blew aft in our faces; astern, our wake was a phosphorescent trail. Long before we expected, the elevated plateau of Shirley Heights loomed over the bow, forcing us to slow still more. After flattening down the mizzen and trimming the jib to windward, we lashed the helm hard alee.

Now we lay at an angle to the oncoming crests, almost without headway. Miraculously the seas seemed to smooth, and like a resting sea bird *Finisterre* swooped up and down, decks dry, the song of wind in the rigging a lullaby. "Heaving to," as the maneuver is commonly called, has been practiced since the earliest days of sail, to slow a vessel in dangerous waters, or to ride out especially heavy weather.

As the moon set and the sun climbed above the Atlantic to reverse the parade of colors of the evening before, we could make out the narrow cut leading into English Harbour, perhaps the most moving reminder of vanished wind ships still in existence. Nelson, Rodney, and Hood had warped their warships through the winding entrance to lie snug within, safe from hurricanes and enemy fleets, while their crews rested and their vessels were refitted. For over a century English Harbour was the key to British naval power in the Caribbean.

As we made a final turn past Berkeley Fort, I stared in disbelief. Eighteen years before when I had entered in *Carib*, the

TED SPIEGEL, RAPHO GUILLUMETTE (ABOVE) AND NATIONAL GEOGRAPHIC PHOTOGRAPHER WINFIELD PARKS

Landlocked monument to vanished wind ships, English Harbour today offers sheltered refuge for cruising yachts. Standing off the island, *Finisterre* (left) waits beneath a lowering moon for dawn to reveal Antigua's narrow gateway.

buildings were ruins, with brickwork crumbling and roofs fallen in, and we had shared the anchorage with a single native sloop.

Now a forest of masts surrounded the stone quays, and on going ashore I found the dockyard looking much as it must have when pigtailed seamen walked there. Behind were grouped buildings with romantic names: the Master Shipwright's House, Galley, Saw Pit, Copper and Lumber Store, Forge, Blacksmith's Shop, Paint Store and Cells, and the Cordage, Canvas and Clothing Store — goods and services essential to a "bundle of sticks held together by strings," as Jack Tar referred to his ship.

It was not long before I learned the

reason for this transformation. In 1947, the same year as my previous visit, a report to the Colonial Office in London described the state of the dockyard as "deplorable."

To save the yard from utter decay, the Governor of the Leeward Islands, Sir Kenneth Blackburne, K.C.M.G.,O.B.E., founded the Society of The Friends of English Harbour in 1951. Winter visitors and devotees of sail on both sides of the Atlantic responded with contributions, even the British royal family assisting, while crews from visiting naval ships gave up their leaves to form work parties.

John Christian, who since 1962 has supervised maintenance and repair work, told me, "By searching Admiralty files in London, the original plans of these buildings were unearthed, just as they were drawn and approved by the architects and engineers. We were able to find carpenters right on Antigua who had retained the skills of the 18th-century shipwrights, familiar

with the same tools. We came very close to duplicating the original work down to the last detail. Even the beams were hewn by hand with adzes, and pegged with wood instead of nailed."

As the abandoned base was reborn it became a haven for a new generation of sailors, partly because of its discovery after the war by retired Comdr. Vernon E. B. Nicholson, O.B.E., of the Royal Navy.

"I sailed out from England with my family in the schooner *Mollihawk* for a holiday," he said as we sat in his office on the quay, masts visible through every window, "but we were also looking for a nugget. Though we came into English Harbour before restoration work had begun, we felt we had found something terrific.

"We offered *Mollihawk* for charter, and to our amazement, we were besieged. The next year we added a second vessel, a ketch. Later we began acting as brokers for other owners, some of whom were on their way

Nelson's Dockyard: Where British frigates moored, pleasure craft make fast to cannon barrels embedded in the quay. Only pillars remain of the Boat House; a hurricane ripped off its roof in 1871. Horatio Nelson, hero of Trafalgar, served here as a captain from 1784 to 1787.

round the world but wanted to make a few pounds. Now I go to the Mediterranean to recruit vessels, and we operate a fleet of about 43 yachts."

The saga of the Nicholsons is part of the story of modern English Harbour. Commander Nicholson took his two sons along for a crew on *Mollihawk*'s first charter. When the business grew, Commander Nicholson stayed behind to handle the burgeoning correspondence, and sons Rodney and Desmond stayed afloat.

After the formation of The Friends of English Harbour, roving yachts began coming in for a look, among them Irving Johnson's *Yankee* on the final leg of a globe-circling voyage. Aboard was an American girl who later became Rodney's wife, going along as cook on charters until a family began to arrive. Desmond also married a daughter of one of the charterers, and she too signed on as cook for the first years of their married life.

Now Commander and Mrs. Nicholson look down on a growing fleet of yachts and grandchildren from the terrace of an 18th-century powder magazine that they have converted into a house oriented to the sea. Even the floors are caulked like a ship's deck, with "scuppers" so water can run off after a scrubbing.

From our snug anchorage at English Harbour we made daily automobile trips to other parts of Antigua. Except for Grande Terre on Guadeloupe, it had so little resemblance to the islands we had already visited it might have been an ocean away. Flat and reef-girt, it has a shoreline of scalloped bays and white sand beaches, and clouds never seem to gather overhead.

During our stay in Dominica we thought there must be an invisible pipeline to the

sky, but on Antigua we had trouble finding enough fresh water for a shower, and were not able to fill *Finisterre*'s tanks. While less than 100 miles away the forests above Roseau are drenched with 360 inches of rain each year, the average fall on Antigua is only 42 inches.

Yet the silver lining for the Antiguan's rare raincloud is almost perpetual sunshine, inviting escape to the tropics when skies turn gray at home. "Tourists are supplanting sugar as our chief crop," said a businessman from St. John's, the capital city. "Our airfield can take the biggest jets. We have 23 hotels and guesthouses, and more are under construction."

Nevertheless, fields of cane make most of the roads unroofed tunnels, with occasional vistas of blue sea beyond the green sea of waving stalks. Ships come from England to carry away the harvest, and St. John's retains much of its colonial character.

Interisland trading sloops and schooners anchor off the waterfront market, but the harbor water is so shallow they must lie well out. A brisk traffic by dinghy and water taxi results. Government House still stands majestically on a wide lawn dotted by palms, although it no longer controls the destiny of the Leeward Islands. But everywhere

Figurehead from H.M.S. *Atalanta* stands among English Harbour mementos in Admiral's House, now a dockyard museum and popular attraction

for visitors to Antigua. A youngster chins on a capstan; sailors of a bygone era labored at the drums, spooling in lines to careen ships.

Swirling cattle egrets prey on snails and insects exposed by a slashing machete in a field of sugar cane

with the old is mixed the new—even the future, since Antigua plays a vital role in the U. S. space program.

Win and I presented ourselves at a guarded gate and soon were greeted by Capt. Richard D. Besley of the U. S. Air Force, who put us in a station wagon for a trip to Mars—or so it seemed to me as we came upon unearthly structures.

"The Antigua Missile Tracking Station is a key link in the Atlantic Missile Range," Captain Besley said. "Antigua is especially important because of its distance from Cape Kennedy, about 1,400 miles; the powered portion of upper stages commences or finishes within our area of view. We are also a command relay station. A submarine cable leading to Cape Kennedy allows the monitors there to turn off a

missile's 'destruct system' after it is clear of land areas, or to relay other command signals," he said.

As he spoke we approached a weird structure that looked like a huge silver spider web balanced atop a slim tower. Cows and donkeys grazed placidly at the base of this telemetry antenna. The combination seemed so far-fetched that I laughed. "Grazing was part of the deal to let the United States use 600 acres," Captain Besley explained. "The Antiguans reserved the right to let their livestock feed where it did not interfere with operations. This piece of equipment is so sensitive that it can pick up electronic noise from galaxies of stars thousands of light-years away—doesn't seem to bother the donkeys, though."

At the other end of the time scale was

The island's chief crop grows on some 12,000 acres.

TED SPIEGEL, RAPHO GUILLUMETTE

the work of Fred Olsen, a retired chemical engineer and amateur archeologist. After coming to Antigua he became interested in the original inhabitants. Fred was born in England of Norwegian and English parents, and during World War I had been lent by the Canadian Government to the United States as an explosives expert. He later became vice-president for research of Olin Mathieson Chemical Corporation. "Now I spend my time on the trail of the Arawak Indians," he said with a smile.

He took me to the site of an Arawak settlement just a few hundred yards from his house at Mill Reef, now a luxurious residential resort. "Not long after moving here I asked myself what a tribe would want in an encampment," he said, "and I decided there were five requirements.

"First, they would need an offshore reef for fishing. Second, a sand beach for pulling up canoes. Third, a source of water. Fourth, a hummock to shelter them from the wind. And fifth, flat land for growing manioc, from which cassava cakes were made. When I found a site combining these features, I began to dig. This is what I found."

In the vertical side of an excavation within sight of the road were embedded shells, some scraps of pottery, fishbones, and even the rim of a pottery griddle used for baking. "You are looking at an Arawak kitchen midden," Fred explained. "Radiocarbon tests place the upper deposits at about A.D. 1100, but deeper layers go back another 700 years. We have recovered about 230,000 potsherds and other things giving a picture of how the Arawaks lived.

"Until the Caribs got this far up the chain, not long before Columbus arrived, it must have been a rather idyllic life. The Arawaks ate well, not only on fish. You can see from these shells they also dined on whelks and conchs, and here is a piece of turtle shell next to a crab claw.

"They varied their diet with birds and cassava bread," Fred continued. "And they enjoyed the same natural features we enjoy today—in fact, you can say that what made a good site for a pre-Columbian tribal settlement is frequently good for a modern resort community!"

Each day, after outings around the island, I returned to English Harbour with a feeling of gratitude, partly because of a pleasant oasis tucked away in one corner of the dockyard. Completed in 1788, the Engineers' Offices of Nelson's day have been converted into a hostelry appropriately called the Admiral's Inn.

FROM comfortable chairs on the terrace we viewed the moored fleet, framed by the stone pillars of the former Boat House. Inside, we dined under hand-hewn beams in an atmosphere admirably in keeping with the restoration.

Alan White, the manager of the inn when I was there, did not neglect the lighter side of island life. One afternoon we were treated to a goat race, when children from the nearby village brought their pets to compete on the terrace. The goats—and a few sheep, as ringers—were dressed in carnival splendor, even to lipstick and

121

NATIONAL GEOGRAPHIC PHOTOGRAPHER WINFIELD PARKS (ABOVE) AND HARRISON FORMAN

Inches from the floor, a limbo dancer contorts his body and wriggles under a flaming bar in an island night club. Dancing couples (above) swing to the rhythm of a steel drum band at the Admiral's Inn. Completed in 1788, it provided storerooms and offices for the English Harbour engineers.

Deep blue of the Caribbean invades the transparent waters of shallow Dickinson Bay. With little rainfall, Antigua counts sunshine and sand among its greatest assets. This mile-long curve of beach alone affords two hotels.

Spurred by their owners, goats sprint for prizes. A gay, flapping costume fails to hamper the leader.

NATIONAL GEOGRAPHIC PHOTOGRAPHER WINFIELD PARKS

wristwatches. Later, on Saturday night, couples danced under the stars to the music of a steel band reverberating from the fortified hillsides.

The earliest reference to English Harbour appears in a letter of 1671 from Sir Charles Wheler, Governor of the Leeward Islands, to the Council for Foreign Plantations in London. He expressed "Hopes the King will think of Antigua; 'tis as large as Barbados & the best land in the West Indies; Falmouth and English Harbours, divided only by a neck of land . . . are so land locked as to be out of danger of hurricanes."

By 1704 defensive works—Berkeley Fort—were built at the entrance we had sailed past, and by 1707 the advice of Sir Charles had been taken by the Navy. The 44-gun ship *Adventure* careened here by heaving herself down with the weight of her own cannon, much as local fishing boats still careen with ballast and tackle.

*E*NGLISH HARBOUR reached its zenith at the end of the 18th century. By then the dockyard could service almost any need of the men-of-war warping through the entrance in a constant stream. Ashore were quarters for officers and crews, along with a galley and a "sickhouse."

Enormous cisterns provided water, and fortifications extended from a chain stretched across the entrance each night in time of war, to gun emplacements commanding every approach. More than 1,000 troops, including artillerymen, formed the shore guard. Even a member of the royal family lived there. In 1787 Clarence House was completed on a hillside opposite the dockyard for H.R.H. Prince William Henry, Duke of Clarence, who became King William IV, the "Sailor King."

Despite English Harbour's martial history, only once was a shot fired in anger, and only once was an attack attempted. In 1798 two young officers—Thomas Pitt, the second Baron Camelford, and Charles Peterson—got into a heated argument as to who had the duty that night. One had to row guard in the harbor, and both wanted to go to a ball. Each claimed to be the senior officer and ordered the other to remain on the station.

After a furious argument, during which each mustered men under his command, Lord Camelford demanded for a final time

if Lieutenant Peterson refused to obey his orders. Upon his reply, "I do!"—Lord Camelford shot his rival dead. Tried and acquitted, the young peer later ended a turbulent career by being killed in a duel.

The attempted attack took place in 1803 when the Governor of French Guadeloupe dispatched 700 men in 13 schooners to carry out a surprise assault. They did not even get near enough for the shore batteries to go into action. A cruising frigate, H.M.S. *Emerald,* intercepted the fleet in the channel, captured three vessels, and sent the rest scurrying.

English Harbour in the 18th century was a crowded and lively place, an endless pageant. Horatio Nelson, then the young captain of H.M.S. *Boreas,* sailed across from here to neighboring Nevis to woo and win a bride given in marriage by the Duke of Clarence. Admiral Rodney, after making himself master of the Dutch island of Statia in 1781, sent some of the captured material to Antigua, and a large brass flowerpot of Dutch origin now in Clarence House is probably part of that booty.

In such surroundings, it is easy to recapture the past. One day as I walked by the Officers' Quarters with maintenance supervisor John Christian, he said musingly, "It is not surprising that people who can see ghosts see them here.

"I think I saw one myself for the first time in my life. Late one afternoon in my bedroom I put down a book and before me stood an officer dressed in the uniform of Nelson's day—dark blue cutaway coat, white stock, pigtail, and all. He was in profile, and I saw him put his hand to his face and cough nervously. The poor chap looked exactly like a man preoccupied with problems, about to have an unpleasant interview.

"Later I found from old drawings that the building called the Admiral's House did not exist when Nelson was stationed here between 1784 and 1787. His house was actually on the site of the present Officers' Quarters. So I'm convinced I saw a ghost who came to be ticked off by the boss!"

Sea-carved Devil's Bridge funnels spray from Atlantic rollers that surge against Antigua's northeast coast. Cautious visitors hold hands for safety on the rugged ledge. The low-lying island rises only 1,300 feet at its highest point.

IX *Montserrat and Nevis: Mountains to the Clouds*

Wearing a misty tiara, a volcanic peak rises on Nevis, once "Queen of the Caribbees." Freight lighter▐

THE COURSE for Nevis was due west. We had turned the corner. Behind us islands stretched in a gentle arc to the shoulder of South America, and now those lying over the bow slanted toward Florida. Turning the corner also put the wind astern. Ever since we left Grenada the trades had blown on the beam, or somewhat ahead, but now *Finisterre* rolled along wing and wing, the main boom on one side, the mizzen on the other.

A faint haze astern began to swallow Antigua, and Nevis became clearer on the horizon ahead; the island of Montserrat rode on our port beam. Because of rough seas and lack of a sheltered harbor at Montserrat I had decided to omit it from our cruise itinerary, but a few days before I had paid it a sentimental visit.

Win and I had gone over by plane from Antigua on a flight billed as one of the world's shortest scheduled routes. In 15 minutes we had vaulted the 35-mile-wide channel and landed on a seaside airstrip.

Once I had stayed a week at Government House in Montserrat as the guest of Charlesworth Ross, the Acting Administrator. So, on arriving, Win and I took a taxi to Plymouth, the capital. Montserrat, except where it is Irish, seems to me as English as it is possible for a British colony to be.

The island is divided into parishes: St. Anthony, St. George's, and St. Peter, but somehow St. Patrick has been slighted.

ait on a sun-flecked sea beside a low-lying arm of St. Kitts. A narrow strait separates the two islands.

There is a St. Patrick's village on the southwest coast, to be sure, near O'Garra's Estate and Galway's Soufrière, a reminder that the Irish settled on Montserrat in the 1630's. Later, during Cromwellian times, other Irish arrived, many as exiles. In some rural areas the brogue lingers as a reminder of the Ould Sod, coming as a surprise to a visitor asking directions of a dusky islander.

Standing at Government House, I had a moment of nostalgia. All was as I remembered it: the sentry box at the gate, the small round garden filled with tropical blooms, the rusted cannon pointing toward the harbor, the green mansion set off by white railings, shutters, and columns.

I could see the vine-screened veranda where Maude Ross and I had watched while Charlesworth ceremoniously carved "the joint," and I knew that upstairs the guestroom must have remained the same. It was a cavernous high-ceilinged room where winged creatures zoomed against the mosquito netting after I blew out the lamp, and where I carefully tapped my shoes on the floor each morning to make sure they harbored no visitors of the night.

Later, as Win and I drove around the island, I found that Government House was one of the few things unchanged. Montserrat was enjoying its own tourist boom. It had five hotels, and along newly bulldozed roads a development company was advertising building lots.

Michael S. Osborne, who has built 24 cottages around his Vue Pointe Hotel to rent to visitors, told me, "Montserrat was once the 'Garden Island of the West Indies.' But—due to the mass emigration to England by 4,500 of our working people in the years 1954 to 1960—the production of tomatoes and sea-island cotton fell to a minimum. An attempt is being made to re-establish the lime industry. It was the juice

An islander models for artist Eva Wilkin in a studio where iron rollers once crushed sugar cane. The converted mill, last of its kind to operate on Nevis, ceased production in 1940.

Time-ravaged ruin of Eden Brown Estate, built for a planter's daughter, was abandoned when her bridegroom died after a wedding-eve duel.

of limes issued by the Royal Navy to prevent scurvy that gave British sailors—and later every Englishman traveling abroad—the nickname 'Limey.'"

When the road left the sea, we found small huts clinging to almost vertical hillsides. Craning my neck to see up towering slopes and down into valleys, I was reminded of an anecdote Charlesworth Ross told to describe the contours of Montserrat: "One day I met a woman with her arm in a sling. I asked her, 'Bridget, what happened?' and she answered, 'Yer honor, I wuz warkin' in me field when I fell out and broke me arrm on the road, begorra!'"

From the deck of *Finisterre*, as we rolled along, Montserrat looked like a vest-pocket Dominica, steep and lush, with spring-fed streams rushing down the mountainsides. Yet I did not regret omitting Montserrat from our cruise itinerary, remembering the port town of Plymouth.

I had stood on the shore with spray blowing in my face from surf breaking on the black sand beach. Offshore a two-masted schooner wallowed, tugging at her anchors, while before me lay the wreck of an island trading vessel that had dragged ashore. At that moment, it had been no place for a small cruiser.

As Montserrat moved astern, Nevis grew plainer ahead. From our deck we saw the symmetrical peak and a hovering cloud that looked like snow. As we moved closer, the illusion of snow turned into a cream puff of cloud and the slopes beneath were a checkerboard of green and yellow fields. Conical stone towers, the bases of windmills once used for crushing sugar cane, dotted the landscape.

I think of Nevis, more than any other island, as symbolizing the sugar economy of the 18th and early 19th centuries, an era doomed by Britain's abolition of slavery in

129

1834. Just as English Harbour represented the zenith of British sea power in the Caribbean before the introduction of steam, so had Nevis sugar estates gained acclaim for the island as "Queen of the Caribbees."

We anchored off Charlestown, and ashore I telephoned an old friend, Mary Pomeroy, one of the most unusual women I have met. Of pure Arab blood, although her father is an English knight, Mary was born on the Mediterranean island of Malta. She studied ballet in a Russian school, worked in London as a decorator, and during the war served as an underground radio operator for British intelligence in Italy.

Finally she visited Nevis and was so enchanted that she bought a plantation and a house built by William Nisbet in 1778—not long before Capt. Horatio Nelson sailed in aboard H.M.S. *Boreas* to court and marry the widowed Frances Nisbet. Deciding visitors would like to stay in a historic mansion, Mary took a course in hotel management at Cornell University and opened Nisbet Plantation as a guesthouse.

When I phoned from Charlestown she was not surprised. The "coconut wireless" of island gossip travels faster than a sailing vessel. That night while candlelight gleamed on the polished mahogany and silver of the dining room at Nisbet's, Mary commented sadly, "The last links with the past are almost gone. Tomorrow I will show you what remains of the great houses and the plantations. Now only four descendants of the old families are still living on Nevis, and they have no children."

Our first stop next morning was Clay Ghaut Estate. The word "ghaut" is often found on islands where indentured East Indian laborers were introduced; I was told that it was their word for ravine or small stream. I had met the owner of Clay Ghaut, Miss Eva Wilkin, on my earlier visit, and this time she waited to welcome us at the door of a windmill tower converted into a studio. Surrounded by her paintings, she reconstructed for me the final workings of the last sugar estate on Nevis.

"We carried on until 1940, when labor difficulties and mechanized competition became too much. Wind spun the vanes above. Gears with cogs of lignum vitae—a very hard wood—turned iron rollers that had been brought out long ago in a sailing ship. The cane was crushed in this room,

Supple cricketer whirls like a pinwheel as he bowls a fast ball during practice on Montserrat. Training on village fields produces internationally famous trophy teams in the West Indies, where cricket ranks high among island sports.

Small spectator maintains wide-eyed interest in track events without missing a bite of ice cream. A rooter at a Montserrat meet, he watched girls skip to the ribbon with jump ropes (right). Earlier contestants raced with soda bottles balanced atop their heads.

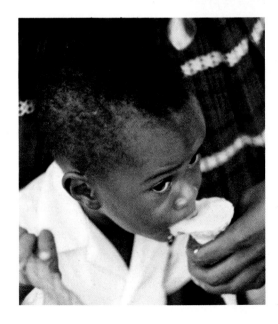

and the juice ran through wooden troughs to an outside shed into large kettles fired by bagasse, the refuse of the stalks.

"After thickening, the juice was ladled into slatted wooden trays to cool. When the molasses dripped away it left muscovado—raw sugar—retaining much of the color and taste of molasses. Because by our methods it was impossible to remove all the moisture, it had to be shipped in barrels instead of sacks. Once almost every estate made its own sugar the same way. Today we buy it in paper bags at the grocery."

Part of the 210 acres remaining of Clay Ghaut borders on Fawcett Estate. "Alexander Hamilton's mother was born there," Miss Wilkin explained as we stood looking over the fields. "She was Rachael Fawcett, said to have been of French Huguenot extraction." Later in Charlestown, we saw the site believed to be Alexander Hamilton's

birthplace. There a plaque commemorates him as "one of the founding fathers of the United States of America."

Nevis in shape is very close to a perfect cone, with the peak sloping down almost evenly on all sides, reminding me of a hoop skirt. As we drove along the main road, we glimpsed a succession of lovely vistas. Once cane had carpeted the lower slopes, with the great houses set back from the water. Just as I was wishing I might get some idea of how it had looked, Mary swung into the drive of Old Manor Estate, the finest example of colonial Georgian architecture on the island.

We entered a room of majestic proportions to meet Bertie Croney, another of the vanishing Nevisians of an old family. He was sitting in a planter's chair, which looked like a canvas deck chair except that the armrests extended several feet, forming a

paneled, others with the remains of brocaded fabric peeling from the walls.

In the back a sunken patio garden, protected from the wind, revealed an intricate pattern of weed-choked beds bordered by stone walks. At one side stood a detached stone kitchen, for in colonial days all West Indian kitchens were separated from the main house to avoid the heat from wood and charcoal fires. Entering a stone-flagged room, we found a fireplace big enough to roast a spitted ox with space left to cook lesser courses.

Farther along the coast road, facing Antigua, Mary pointed to a ruin that stood out from the green hillside like a bleached skull: "Eden Brown Estate was built by a wealthy planter as a wedding present for his daughter and furnished lavishly with English furniture, Georgian silver, fine linen, and Crown Derby porcelain.

Dashing Capt. Horatio Nelson wooed a young Nevis widow while serving at English Harbour. A faded entry in the Fig Tree Church marriage register records the success of his courtship: "1787. March 11th. Horatio Nelson, Esquire, Captain of his Majesty's Ship, the Boreas, to Frances Herbert Nesbit, Widow." The mansion on Montpelier Estate, scene of the wedding, has vanished. So has the house nearby where, according to tradition, Alexander Hamilton was born. A plaque (left) commemorates the American statesman. It gives his birth date as 1757, two years later than that favored by many scholars.

comfortable footrest. Leaning back with his legs sprawled, he invited us to join him, and as the trade wind whistled through jalousies, we looked past the ruins of a sugar factory to Montserrat. Cheerfully Bertie told us there was hope Old Manor would be saved—an American investor contemplated transforming it into a guesthouse, even making the former rainwater catchment a swimming pool.

Afterward, we followed Bertie through the house. Our footsteps rang on marble floors, and, despite the bright sunshine, a dim and ghostly quality pervaded the place. Through open doors I glimpsed other rooms, almost bare of furniture, some

"The night before the marriage, the bridegroom got into a drunken argument with his best man. They dueled with pistols at dawn and both were killed. The girl went to England, and her father sealed the house. It was never lived in."

Nevis has famous springs which used to be the most fashionable thermal cure outside Europe. The first known reference to them appears in the works of Captain John Smith, who dropped anchor here in 1607 on his way to Virginia. His company came ashore to fill water casks and replenish the wood for the galley fire.

In the course of their exploration, several of the crew presumably touched the leaves of manchineel trees, which have an effect similar to that of poison ivy. (Caribs dipped their arrow points in the sap to make them more potent.) Fortunately the victims later "found a great Poole, wherein bathing themselves, they found much ease . . . [and] were well-cured in two or three dayes."

Later travelers reported similar relief for almost every ailment suffered by man, from gout to leprosy, and when the Bath House Hotel was built in the 18th century, it became internationally known. Visitors arrived not only from other West Indian islands but also from Britain—no mean compliment when the round-trip voyage took weeks.

Resisting time, hurricanes, and earthquakes, the Bath House is still impressive, though no longer open to guests. Built at a reputed cost of £40,000—an enormous amount during the days of slave labor—it towers above modern Charlestown, with its thick stone walls, vaulted roof, and wide verandas. The baths, fed by hot springs, maintain a constant temperature of 108° F., and the water on analysis closely resembles

that of the famous thermal springs of Württemberg in Germany.

Charlestown itself bears out the theme of vanished glory. Almost leveled by fire in 1873, the town was rebuilt partly in stone and partly in wood, and almost invariably with corrugated steel roofs. Donkeys share the streets with automobiles. Natural crooks cut from trees—the same that form the frames of local boats—support many upper verandas of homes.

Overlooking a small triangular "square," the Court House recalls black days in the career of Horatio Nelson. Here merchants instigated a case against him for £4,000. Nelson, then a Captain, rigidly interpreted an act that restricted the rebellious North American colonies from trading in the West Indies. An unpopular law, it was largely ignored by government officials and even by other officers of the Royal Navy.

So when Nelson intercepted four American ships off Nevis in 1785, the irate Nevisians, considering this virtually an act of piracy against their property aboard, persuaded the American ship captains to sue for damages. The President of the Nevis Council, a Mr. Herbert, offered to stand Nelson's £10,000 bail. The Admiralty sustained the Captain, but his popularity with the islanders reached a low ebb.

Nevertheless, with the aplomb he was to show right down to his death in the cockpit of *Victory* at the Battle of Trafalgar, Nelson went about his business. He paced Saddle Hill each day with his spyglass, and even wooed a local lady.

In the register of Fig Tree Church, not far out of Charlestown, we deciphered an entry in faded ink on crumbling paper: "1787. March 11th. Horatio Nelson, Esquire, Captain of his Majesty's Ship, the Boreas, to Frances Herbert Nesbit, Widow." The marriage took place in the great house of Montpelier Estate, now vanished. A future king of England, the Duke of Clarence, sailed over from English Harbour to give the bride away.

With streamers of fireworks — and bright fabrics — Montserrat celebrates the first visit of its sovereign. The royal yacht *Britannia* (right) brought Queen Elizabeth II and Prince Philip into Plymouth harbor, where costumed islanders waited to perform in their honor on February 19, 1966.

X St. Kitts:
Sugar From the Fields

Trailing a boiling wake, *Finisterre* reaches across The Narrows off St. Kitts. Early British and Frenc

S T. KITTS AND NEVIS could be called sister islands, but, to be historically exact, mother and daughter would be better. For St. Christopher, better known by its nickname, was the site of the first permanent English colony in the Caribbean.

Captain Thomas Warner landed in 1624 with his wife and eldest son and about 13 settlers to challenge fate—which took the form of fierce Caribs, Spaniards jealously protecting their "lake," undergrowth to be cut before cultivation could begin, and tropical diseases. The colony prospered and sent out shoots to other islands, beginning with Nevis. St. Kitts is therefore the Mother Isle of the British West Indies.

As *Finisterre* boiled across The Narrows, I noted in the log, "Best sail of the winter!"

Nowhere did the sea seem a deeper blue or the clouds a purer white. St. Kitts, like Nevis, is lovely, tapering from a culminating peak to a coastal plain.

Standing by the main shrouds while Henry steered, I had both St. Kitts and Nevis in sight and was reminded of other paired islands I had seen from the deck of a small cruiser: Tahiti and Moorea in the Pacific, Ischia and Capri in the Mediterranean, all different but all conveying the same sharp stab of beauty.

Although at the narrowest point the channel is only two miles wide, it is 13 miles between Charlestown and Basseterre. Win and Mary Pomeroy had flown across. They landed long before we dropped anchor off Basseterre amid a fleet of beamy craft used

ettlers on the island drove out the Carib Indians—and were in turn banished for a time by a Spanish fleet.

NATIONAL GEOGRAPHIC PHOTOGRAPHER WINFIELD PARKS

to ferry sugar cane from Nevis. Going ashore, I was surprised to be greeted by the driver of an official limousine and whisked off to Government House. There I found Win and Mary enjoying the hospitality of Lt. Col. Henry Howard, Administrator of St. Kitts, Nevis, and Anguilla. He became our guide, mentor, and firm friend.

"I come from a line whose ladies tend to lose their heads," Henry said jokingly not long after we had met. "Catherine Howard was the fifth wife of Henry VIII, and Anne Boleyn's mother was also a Howard. But I'll try to stay intact while I show you round."

Henry had spent part of his childhood in Washington, where his father was British Ambassador, and part on the family estate of Greystoke in Cumberland, England. At Greystoke he hunted on a knoll named Bunker Hill by an ancestor, the 11th Duke of Norfolk, who was a strong supporter of the colonists in their struggle for independence. "So you see," he laughed, "I grew up part American." St.

Kitts was Henry's final colonial post before retirement, but he has assured himself of remaining in the West Indies by buying land on Anguilla, the most northerly of the three islands under his administration.

We had not been long on St. Kitts before *Finisterre* acquired a new crew member, Melville Bell Grosvenor, President and Editor of the National Geographic Society. He and I had often been shipmates, going back to the days of *Carib,* my first ocean cruiser. An experienced sailor and a skipper himself, Mel would be a welcome fourth hand for the longer open-water sailing that lay ahead.

St. Kitts seemed like a carefully tended garden, and indeed it is. Its Carib name was Liamuiga, the "Fertile Isle," and for over three centuries descendants of settlers have worked the fields. Sugar cane grows in a broad belt around Mount Misery and the lesser peaks forming the central spine. Approximately 16,000 acres—more than one-third of the total land area—are under

Sails shot full of holes, French ships vainly attack British men-of-war that block them from their base on St. Kitts. In the battle in 1782, Comte de Grasse found himself tricked out of position by Sir Samuel Hood, who feigned retreat to provoke pursuit, then suddenly sailed back to cut off his enemy. Impressive but futile, Hood's feat failed to achieve his goal of lifting the siege of Brimstone Hill Fort (map, below).

cultivation, and production has exceeded 50,000 tons of sugar and 1,500,000 gallons of molasses during good years.

A narrow-gauge railway carries cane to a central factory, which extracts the juice by modern machinery. So dominant is sugar in the island economy that it accounts for about 90 percent of the foreign earnings. Other sugar islands, such as Barbados and Antigua, have the cushion of tourist revenue, but as sugar goes—a notoriously unstable commodity on the world market—so goes St. Kitts. The estates have experimented with other crops but have always come back to their traditional planting, and vegetables and fruit must still be imported from Nevis to supplement local production.

At the center of Basseterre is a monument that honors a departed dignitary of the Victorian era, the Honourable Thomas Berkeley. It is an ornamental structure of columns and iron curlicues, topped by four clocks, each facing a different quadrant of the compass, so citizens may always know

Mt. Misery
3792 feet

ST. CHRISTOPHER
(ST. KITTS)

Caribbean Sea

Brimstone
Hill Fort

Basseterre

ROUTE OF
FINISTERRE

The Narrows

NEVIS

Caribbean Sea

Charlestown

N

139

the time. Yet I confess I've often regarded these reminders of passing hours with as little time-consciousness as I have known anywhere in the world, for overlooking the clocks is the balcony of the leisurely Palms Hotel, successor to Shorty's, my headquarters during *Carib* days.

The Palms remains a hostelry in the West Indian tradition, as opposed to the glass-and-chrome air-conditioned structures of recent origin. Napkin rings beside places in the dining room give guests a feeling of permanence, even in transit. Sugar bowls stand in plates of water to guard against ants, mesh covers in the kitchen discourage other insects, and the waitress ambles to your table at a pace to soothe any traveler not catching an airplane. Tea and cocktails on the veranda are a relaxed ritual, while high-ceilinged rooms dark behind jalousied windows invite siestas.

Sallying forth on the day after our arriv-al, I turned right at the old Treasury Building to walk along the waterfront, which was like an oriental bazaar except for surf rushing up the black sand beach. Some women had set up tables and booths, others had simply spread their goods out on the sidewalk. They displayed everything from plastic bracelets and bangles stamped out in Manchester or Osaka factories to patiently handcrafted local products: brooms of palm fronds, woven mats of coconut fiber, clay cooking pots and charcoal braziers, sea salt in huge sparkling crystals. I asked a vendor where the salt came from, and she pointed toward the jutting point of St. Kitts nearest Nevis. "They's salt ponds behind White House Bay," she said. "It's like a desert. Ain't no rain from one month to another."

As I left the waterfront, I reread from my notebook a description of Basseterre that I had jotted down earlier. It had been

"Gibraltar of the West Indies": The garrison of Brimstone Hill Fort gained glory even while losing the only battle it fought. In 1782 a British force of about 1,200 men withstood 6,000 attacking Frenchmen for nearly a month. The courage of the defenders so impressed the French that after the fort fell they let the king's troops go with flags flying. Visitors (below) stand on the ramparts. Statia rises in the distance.

FRED WARD, BLACK STAR

published by a Mr. Blome in 1672. I found it still an almost perfect description: "... A Town of a good bigness, whose Houses are well built, of Brick, Freestone, and Timber; where the Merchants have their Store-houses, and is Inhabited by Tradesmen, and are well served with such Commodities, both for the Back, and Belly, together with Utensils for their Houses, and Plantations, as they have occasion of.... Here is a fair, and large Church, as also a publique-Hall, for the administration of Justice: Here is also a very fair Hospital...."

Walking through the streets of the business district, I found the stores not only stocked with "Commodities, both for the Back, and Belly," but also with "Utensils for their Houses" that Mr. Blome could not have imagined—displays of electrical appliances ranging from refrigerators to washing machines. Competing merchants offered a variety of goods I had not seen equaled on any other island, and even featured window posters inviting time-payment purchase.

The Kittitians are proud of being part of the oldest English settlement in the West Indies, but the island equally deserves the title of "Mother of the French Antilles." Site of a French colony before either Martinique or Guadeloupe, it once managed the affairs of the larger daughters.

Open roadstead of Basseterre throbs with the vending of pottery, charcoal, and vegetables. Vessels stopping here must lie well offshore because of the shallow water. A girl in a multi-striped hat (above) plays beside a boat that carries goods ashore from the anchored merchant ships.

French settlement on St. Kitts began about a year after the English arrived. Thomas Warner had sailed back to England to sell his first crop of tobacco, and some time in 1625 a French ship limped in after fighting a Spanish warship. The Caribs posed a threat to the small colony, so the English allowed the French company to disembark and establish themselves.

Together the Europeans slaughtered the Indians, finally driving the remnants off the island, but they did not have long to rejoice. A Spanish fleet attacked the island in 1629, destroyed the houses and crops, and banished most of the inhabitants.

Some of the refugees sailed downwind to the small island of Tortuga. There they joined outlaws who had been driven from nearby Hispaniola by the Spanish. The settlers earned their living by selling meat to passing vessels. They dried it over fires called *boucans*—giving them the name buccaneers, which lingered long after they had left the island as sea rovers to prey on Spanish shipping. So I like to think that St. Kitts might also claim another title, "Father of the Pirates."

After the Spanish fleet disappeared, the St. Kitts colonies soon re-established themselves, the English taking the center and the French the two ends. The French part of the island was governed by Philippe de

Palms straight as ship's masts circle the clock tower in Basseterre, capital of St. Kitts. Swept by hurricane in 1843, fire in 1867, and flood in 1880, the town endures as a shipping center.

In patchwork fields near Basseterre, a couple runs hand in hand on Bayford Estate. A launch trip tak

Lonvilliers de Poincy, who built a castle in the European manner. For 20 years he lived in almost feudal splendor, administering the entire French West Indies.

Rising above fields of sugar cane and ginger plants, the fortified Château de la Montagne was of brick and cut stone, three stories high, and flanked by gardens watered from a mountain stream. Vivid flags flew from the parapet and upper balconies to celebrate French victories and public holidays, and for special occasions musicians played clarions from the roof.

"Legend has it that by a trick of the echoes, the sound traveled down the valleys, so it could be heard throughout the island," Henry Howard told us as we drove past the ruins of Château de la Montagne. "It is believed that a secret tunnel extended more than two miles from the house to emerge in St. Peter's Church.

"The chateau must have been the wonder of the Caribbee world until it was destroyed by a terrible earthquake about 1689, when the ground opened nine feet in places, swallowing whole sugar mills. But De Poincy gave us something tangible which remains. He introduced the poinciana, which you see flowering everywhere."

A coastal road circles the island, and, as

Sugar field forms a backdrop for brightly dressed families of cane workers just out of church. The crop is vital to St. Kitts' economy.

isitors across The Narrows to nearby Nevis, a daughter colony of St. Kitts settled in the 17th century.

FRED WARD, BLACK STAR (BELOW) AND NATIONAL GEOGRAPHIC PHOTOGRAPHER WINFIELD PARKS

on Antigua, fields of cane press in from either side, offering only an occasional glimpse of the sea. We were driving on a Sunday, and at times families dressed in their best clothes, walking home from church, slowed our car. "I'm taking you to a planter lunch," Henry explained as we turned into a lane leading to Wingfield Manor Estate. There, in the central room, platters and bowls of food crowded a long table, some of them contributions of neighboring estate ladies to a community feast.

Afterward, I joined a group for a climb up a ravine that led to the major source of Basseterre's water supply, a spring on the side of Wingfield Mountain. Lichen-covered rocks broke the flow of a bubbling stream, bordered by ferns, bamboo, and elephant ears, huge drooping green leaves. Sunlight filtered through trees overgrown by air plants and creepers, some as thick as a ship's hawser. The miniature jungle was a surprise among the neat fields.

The entire leeward coast is dominated by Brimstone Hill, the "Gibraltar of the West Indies." Rising almost vertically more than 750 feet above the plain, the outcropping does resemble the Rock. Carib legend maintained that Brimstone Hill was once part of Mount Misery, blown out like a giant plug during a volcanic eruption.

When we climbed to the top of Brimstone we saw another reason for the comparison to Gibraltar — an enormous complex of fortifications designed to be impregnable to the weapons of the day. Thick masonry walls towered above the cliffs, and the few possible approaches were commanded by flanking outworks.

"Military engineers planned Brimstone Hill as a bastion that could never be captured," Henry Howard told us. "Oddly enough, the only time it was attacked, by the French in 1782, it fell. While still under construction, it surrendered to the Marquis de Bouillé and 6,000 seasoned

Liamuiga—the "Fertile Isle," the Caribs called St. Kitts. Scooping freshly cut sugar cane, a long-armed tractor whisks the stalks into carts for loading on railroad cars. Thirty-six miles of narrow-gauge track take the crop to a mill that converts it into sugar and molasses for export.

French troops. The garrison consisted of 1,200 men, but the odds were made even worse by local hostility.

"The Kittitians were said to be so infuriated by Admiral Rodney's pillage of the neighboring Dutch island of Statia the year before—when shipping and stores belonging to the St. Kitts merchants were seized together with Dutch property—they refused to help the British carry up cannon and ammunition from the base of the hill. The besieging French captured these and turned them against the defenders, and for nearly a month concentrated cannon and mortar fire on the summit.

"When the garrison finally surrendered, less than half the troops were fit for duty. The French were so impressed by their bravery that they allowed them the full honors of war, and so the English troops marched out carrying their arms, drums beating and colors flying."

In 1783 the fort came back into English possession, but by the time it was completed the need for it had largely vanished. The focus of military struggle again shifted to Europe. Nevertheless, a garrison remained at the fortress until 1854.

Today Brimstone Hill is comparable to English Harbour, representing the highest development of land fortifications during the same period in the British West Indies. Most of the wooden structures have rotted away, but some of the stone battlements are as solid as when the last mason put down his trowel. And time will never destroy one of the most magnificent panoramas in the world. Below us St. Kitts was dwarfed to the scale of a relief map, and beyond we could see across blue channels to our next island goals, Statia and Saba.

Henry drove us on to Government House, once part of the panoply of a far-flung empire. As we passed a sentry box and stopped before the entrance of a sprawling mansion dating from the time of Queen Victoria, I felt I was stepping into a bygone era.

We walked through tall doors into a foyer, and then into a drawing room opening onto a formal garden. Silver candelabra stood on the buffets in the dining room, flanking a banquet-size dining table. As in other Government Houses, portraits of the royal family appeared at every turn. It seemed part of an ordered world that was, an order that is fast changing, as we had found in our passage through the islands.

"St. Kitts is in the last phase of colonial government before independence," Henry told us. "I am appointed as Administrator by the Queen, along with the Attorney General, but the other five members of the Executive Council are elected by the people. There is a Chief Minister, and the Administrator is bound to accept the advice of his Executive Council, having only one final power in an emergency—the right to suspend the Constitution. The final stage of independence will come when the locally elected government maintains control in all circumstances."

Skipper hails a friend aboard a French ketch bound for Martinique. Editor Grosvenor, at *Finisterre*'s helm, boarded the yawl at St. Kitts for the cruise to St. Thomas in the Virgin Islands.

In return for his hospitality, we invited Henry Howard for an afternoon sail aboard *Finisterre*. To add dignity to the occasion, we borrowed his official Colony flag to fly from the masthead, a Union Jack bearing in its center the arms of St. Christopher-Nevis-Anguilla. When Henry Davis brought the Administrator alongside in the Whaler, Mel Grosvenor, Win Parks, and I lined the rail like the side boys of Nelson's day, apologizing for a lack of skirling bos'n's pipes. There formality ended, as it always does aboard small sailing vessels at the first puff of wind and the first dollop of spray.

Flattening sails to a fresh breeze funneling through The Narrows, we beat across Frigate Bay, scene of a memorable maneuver by British Commodore Sir Samuel Hood against the French fleet commanded by Admiral Comte de Grasse. Capt. Alfred Thayer Mahan described it in *The Influence of Sea Power upon History* as not only standing in "the very first rank of naval battles," but "the most brilliant military effort of the whole war."

It had happened in 1782, a busy year for the rival navies, culminating in the Battle of the Saintes on April 12. The battle might never have taken place and given victory to the British, had not the defenders of Brim-stone Hill held out so gallantly, and had not Hood rounded Nevis Point on the afternoon of January 24 to find De Grasse anchored off Basseterre.

As we sailed the same waters, we talked of the stirring event. When Hood appeared, De Grasse's numerically superior fleet made sail and stood out of the bay, ready for battle. The English turned away and steered south, as though retreating, but staying to windward. Through the night De Grasse remained on the alert. The next day Hood suddenly tacked back toward Basseterre.

De Grasse realized what was happening too late. Hood sailed near the spot De Grasse had vacated, thus putting himself between the French and their shore base, established to assist in the siege of Brimstone Hill. The English ships anchored so they could swing themselves around to reload after each broadside and thus deliver two rounds to the enemy's one.

The French fleet filed past twice but failed to break the British line. De Grasse blockaded the island for nearly a month, then sailed to Martinique to refit his fleet.

In the meantime, Rodney arrived to take up watch at Pigeon Island before he pursued and defeated De Grasse in the Battle of the Saintes.

Next morning *Finisterre*'s crew was on deck before sunrise. With the perfume of frying bacon and brewing coffee sharpening our appreciation of the better things of life, we watched the first rays tint the clouds over Mount Misery while the coast remained wrapped in purple shadows. Soon we scudded past Basseterre, then under the ramparts of Brimstone Hill Fort.

It was hard to imagine, rolling along over dancing water while flying fish skittered past, that the intrigues of power politics had ever brought violence to these sunny isles. Yet lifting higher as we shot each wavecrest loomed Statia, an island that had suffered greatly in the wake of Europe's struggles in the Caribbean.

Flaming royal poinciana unfolds a scarlet umbrella above Brimstone Hill. The tree takes its name from Philippe de Poincy, a French Governor of St. Kitts during the 17th century.

XI *The Dutch Windwards:*
Statia, Saba, St. Maarten

"Rodney's work!" exclaimed a small boy at play among the ruins of once-busy Lower Town, remindin

*D*ROPPING ANCHOR off Statia's Oranjestad we again hoisted our yellow quarantine flag. We could see men sitting under a sea-grape tree beyond surfboats drawn up on the beach. A pall seemed to have settled over the port, an apathy extending from the streets of Upper Town to the boatmen of Lower Town.

It was not always thus. Once St. Eustatius — or Statia, as it is generally called — was one of the busiest ports in the Caribbean. Ships clustered along its narrow bank of soundings, and a stream of lighters and barges shuttled to the beach day and night. Full warehouses built to the water's edge

flanked roistering taverns and sailors' hangouts. On a plateau overlooking the roadstead, merchants lived in imposing homes.

Declared a free port by the Netherlands, Statia in the 18th century had become the crossroads for trade between Europe and America, and among the islands. Ships from Boston or New York could clear for the Netherlands West Indies with cargoes of colonial products desired by English merchants, then meet ships from London or Liverpool loaded with goods desperately needed by the colonists, including munitions used during the Revolutionary War. Statia became the "Golden Rock," reputedly

e author that Statians neither forget nor forgive the British Admiral who pillaged their island in 1781.

NATIONAL GEOGRAPHIC PHOTOGRAPHER WINFIELD PARKS

the wealthiest island of its size in the world.

At the height of its bustle and prosperity, in sailed the American brigantine *Andrew Doria* on November 16, 1776, when the ink was hardly dry on the Declaration of Independence. Rounding to smartly, she dipped her colors, and upon acknowledgment fired a salute to Fort Oranje, capping the hill of Upper Town. There was a pause while Governor Johannes de Graaff made a difficult decision, but then his guns rang out in the first salute by a foreign government to a flag flown by the Continental Navy.

The incident added fuel to the fury of the British Government and its fighting men, but almost five years passed before they could retaliate. Then came a dispatch to Admiral Rodney in Barbados that England had declared war on the Netherlands.

Before the islanders received the news, Rodney pounced with his fleet. The first intimation Governor de Graaff had of hostilities was receipt of an ultimatum from the commanding officers stating that "we . . . demand an instant surrender of the island of St. Eustatius and its dependencies, with every thing in and belonging thereto. . . . We give you one hour from the delivery of this message, to decide. . . ."

De Graaff began his message of capitulation by writing, "Well knowing the honour and humanity of the two commanders," but his optimism was unfounded. Rodney picked the island clean. He carried away goods worth an estimated £3,000,000, according to the valuation of the time.

As the system of "prize money" allowed naval officers a share of captured booty,

First foreign salute to the flag of a warship of the infant United States boomed from Dutch guns on Statia. On November 16, 1776, the *Andrew Doria*, a brigantine of the new Continental Navy, sailed into the harbor below Fort Oranje. After a dipping of colors, the ship fired a salute. The Dutch hesitated, then replied. The incident infuriated the British, and five years later Admiral Rodney sacked Statia. *Finisterre* (below) rolls at anchor in the historic roadstead.

Rodney had a personal interest in the proceedings. He even continued flying the Dutch flag over Fort Oranje for more than a month, adding unwary latecomers to the bag for a total of 150 vessels. Then he destroyed the seawall protecting Lower Town, and burned valuable dyewoods because they could not be transported.

A surfboat finally came out to take us ashore. As we approached, we saw a few roofless stone walls rising above the beach, marking the site of old Lower Town. Trudging up the hillside, we entered Fort Oranje to meet the Administrator, Laurens Rosema, who received us cordially.

He invited us into the living room of his house where decorations were still in place from the visit of Princess Beatrix the preceding week. As I looked about, I was in-

trigued by a television set, for it seemed somehow incongruous on an island which in a previous generation had not even known of a declaration of war for over a month. "What can you pick up?" I asked. The answer came in chorus from the Administrator's two daughters, "Puerto Rico!"

Statia is one of the Netherlands Windward Islands, which lie confusingly among the British Leewards. "There are six islands in the Netherlands Antilles," Mr. Rosema explained. "The southern division is called the 'ABC group'—Aruba, Bonaire, and Curaçao—lying near the coast of South America. They are the Leeward Islands. We are part of the '3-S group'—Statia, Saba, and St. Maarten—and, lying to windward of the ABC group, are officially and correctly the Windwards. The islands are a political

PAINTING BY PHILLIPS MELVILLE

Harboring 200 ships at a time, the port of Oranjestad funneled riches to Statia, shipper for the plantation isles and trading center between Europe and America. The old print errs in placing Fort Oranje at sea level. Actually, the fortification stood on the cliffs above the beach. The island's fortunes waned when trading declined in the 19th century.

entity, and are an equal and integral part of the Kingdom of the Netherlands."

Like Antigua, Statia was suffering from a drought. Beyond ruins of brick houses, some merely stone-arched windows with no walls, I could see parched hillsides. Near the cliff dropping away to the beach stood the remains of a large church whose scale gave an indication of the community it had served.

More than 8,000 people once lived on Statia, contrasted with a current population of 1,214, of whom 350 are school children. Until 1960 the population had dwindled by half as the men sought work in the oil refineries of Curaçao and Aruba. "It reminds me of a western ghost town," Win Parks commented as we passed between stone fences guarding empty yards.

Yet there is hope of a development that will benefit the island. When we left the Administrator's residence a fellow American stopped his jeep to invite us to lunch. He was George A. Bauer, a former captain in the U. S. Army. While stationed in Puerto Rico he and his wife decided that they wanted to continue living in the West Indies, and on their leave visited various islands. Finding the Dutch possessions the most promising because of their virtual freedom from taxes and import levies, Captain Bauer moved his family to Statia.

"We feel there must be others who think as we do," he explained over the luncheon table, "and want a place to live inexpensively away from the pace of the modern world. Here land prices are among the lowest in the West Indies, yet we have the same

Netherlands flag at Fort Oranje flies above a plaque given by President Franklin D. Roosevelt to commemorate the first foreign salute to a U. S. warship. Obelisk honors Dutch Admiral Michiel de Ruyter.

sunshine, trade winds, and blue sea. I have bought a tract outside of Oranjestad, and we will soon build a house there and provide sites for others who might come."

In Fort Oranje I witnessed a scene dating from sailing-ship days. Sitting with the Administrator in his office, I became aware of a babble of voices from the post office next door. I went out to find much of the population of Statia on the veranda and spilling over into the yard. Above the crowd was a postal clerk with a sack of mail.

As he extracted each letter he called the name of the addressee in a loud voice: "Daniel Woodley, Albertis Leverock, Carol van Putten, Leo van Zanten . . ." Each name brought a response: "Here I is!" a voice might shout from the back, and the letter would be passed hand to hand; or a friend

might reply, "She home sick. She say if she get a letter she come fetch it to-morrow;" or, "Give it to me. I'll leave it by!"

Mr. Rosema came out to stand by my side. "This happens twice a week when a mail plane comes from Saba and St. Maarten," he explained. "Statia is the last island in the Netherlands West Indies where mail is distributed like this, but we are small and it works."

From the walls of the fort we could see bottom through the clear water off the beach. "Those dark outlines against the sand are not coral reefs," the Administrator told me, "but the foundations of the warehouses and seawall. Judging from the ruins, Lower Town must have stretched nearly a mile, a long narrow strip between the sea and the high ground."

Faces glowing with affection, students of S▮

Ring-around-the-rosy: Waiting for a bus on French St. Martin, smiling schoolgirls banish boredom with a favorite game.

Follow the leader: St. Martin boys teeter on a palm tree. Later, the salt water of Marigot Bay will soothe sore hands and feet.

All fall down: A winsome water sprite kicks joyfully on the sandy bottom of her natural bubble bath at Zeelandia Beach, Statia.

ozef School, Saba, present birthday bouquets and their prized paintings inscribed "for our sister."

We then passed a reminder of how some of Statia's troubles had begun. At the base of the flagpole in the center of the yard a bronze plaque says, in part: "Here the sovereignty of the U.S.A. was first formally acknowledged to a national vessel by a foreign official. Presented by Franklin Delano Roosevelt, President of the U.S.A."

Before returning to *Finisterre*, Mel Grosvenor had a private talk with the Administrator. So, to my surprise, when we prepared to make evening colors, a police officer manned the Netherlands flag flying above Fort Oranje. We dipped our ensign, and received a salute in return. This time there was no Rodney to disturb the peace.

We relaxed in the cockpit while wonderful aromas wafted from the galley as Henry prepared *poulet á la Finisterre*, chicken sautéed in butter, simmered in stock, and seasoned with herbs and wine. Below, with candles on the table, soft music from hidden speakers, and tropical fruit and French cheeses in reach, we enjoyed one of the best aspects of small-boat cruising—to be at home while sampling the finest from distant lands.

Always, afloat, I made a fetish of dining well, one of the reasons for *Finisterre*'s ocean

racing success, as energy never failed. Hot food had been a secret weapon; we often enjoyed appetizing meals from the swing table when the rest of the fleet was eating beans spooned cold from the can.

On deck for a final look, I saw hardly a glimmer from the houses of Upper Town to show that people still lived there. At sunset, police had made the rounds of the streets, hoisting lanterns on poles, for Statia had no electricity. But I was startled when I looked to the west. Neighboring Saba, which I thought too remote to be touched by modernity, was ablaze with points of light, clustered high on a mountainside. Henry peered through the hatch and exclaimed, "The Saba Hilton!"

For me, Saba has always had a Through the Looking Glass quality. So many legends have evolved around the steep volcanic cone thrusting from the sea that it is hard to separate reality from fantasy. There has never been a harbor, and only recently an airstrip, so Saba has remained one of the least-visited and least-known of the Leewards.

There were tales of a town called The Bottom, though it stood on a mountainside; of boats being built on the heights and lowered to the water; and of a population

157

Lacking beaches or ports, Saba's precipitous slopes plunge to 100-fathom depths only 600 yards offshor

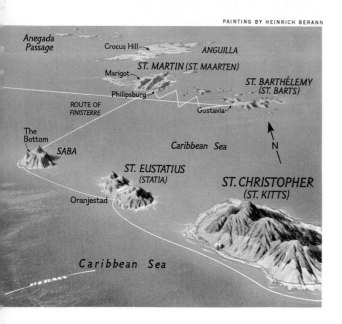

PAINTING BY HEINRICH BERANN

once so predominantly female that Saba was called "the island of women," as the men left to find work elsewhere.

Stars were still bright as we set sail for Saba. At dawn, a silhouette sometimes compared to Napoleon's cocked hat lay close ahead. The slanting rays of early morning sunshine etched in stark relief chasms fissuring the cliffs, bold and forbidding, with surf breaking heavily around the base. Jagged crags seemed to form a stairway from water level to the cloud cover, offering no place for man's habitations. Yet clinging to the rock sides were white blocks of houses, and as I looked through binocu-

International family of islands became pawns in a long European power struggle. By 1816 Statia alone had changed hands 22 times.

Settlers defended their island against pirate attacks by tumbling stones upon the heads of invaders.

lars I saw an automobile crawling around a hairpin curve.

On my cruise in *Carib* I had managed to anchor in Saba's Ladder Bay for several days. But this, I was certain, would be impossible during a winter of such unusually strong winds. I had therefore sent a radio message from Statia to Saba's Administrator requesting that a surfboat stand by at eight o'clock to take off Win Parks and his camera equipment. On schedule, we approached Fort Bay landing.

Watching the boat struggle toward us through breaking seas, I wondered how we could make the transfer. When *Finisterre* was lifting on the crests, the surfboat was plummeting—like two elevators passing in opposite directions. But suddenly the boatmen yelled as the vessels hung poised on the same wave for an instant, and Win, festooned with cameras, tumbled aboard.

Slowly *Finisterre* continued around the western side of Saba, sheltered from the trade winds. Holding in close to the shore, I pointed out The Ladder to Mel, a steep flight of steps cut into the rock. "I counted them when I came down," I told him. "There were over 500—I forget how many, but plenty." Now disused because of the jeep road at Fort Bay landing, Ladder Bay remains the smoothest anchorage of Saba —if the wind doesn't shift. Looking forward to unworried exploration of the heights, I had no regrets at sailing past.

Finisterre repaid us for not tethering her off the bleak shore; as the wind came back, she romped over the seas like a colt galloping across a hilly pasture. We swiftly

reached across the 25-mile channel to the Dutch port of Philipsburg, on St. Maarten. There I planned to leave *Finisterre* with Henry while Mel and I flew back to Saba.

When I first heard that an airstrip had been built on Saba, I exclaimed, "Impossible!" I could not recall a piece of flat land larger than a tablecloth. Yet that afternoon I found myself climbing aboard a Dornier 28, an odd-looking contraption with high undercarriage and parasol wings. "It is of German design," said pilot Jose Dormoy, "developed from planes used for wartime reconnaissance. Through adjustable wing flaps and slots, we can go up and down almost as steeply as a helicopter. See!" With the last word, we shot up so abruptly that the tail wheel banged the runway.

Clouds had gathered, and Saba, as we neared, looked more forbidding than ever. The summit was hidden, but lesser crags appeared through trailing streamers of mist. Suddenly the pilot pointed, and below I saw something that looked like an aircraft carrier's flight deck balanced on a spur of rock, with both ends hanging over the sea. Instead of heading directly for it, the pilot approached a mountainside.

At the last possible moment, he banked the plane sharply, and the wheels touched down. "Have to do it that way with the wind in this direction," the pilot explained casually as we rolled to a stop. I looked at Mel, and Mel looked at me with raised eyebrows. We shared a feeling of thanksgiving as we climbed from the plane and put our feet on the solid rock of Saba.

If the airport is a miracle of engineering, it is only slightly more of one than the road snaking up the mountain to the town of Windwardside, 1,300 feet above the sea. By jeep, we took off almost as steeply as the plane, twisting and climbing until we reached Upper Hell's Gate, a village that could hardly have been more unreal if it had been made of gingerbread.

Neat white cottages with softly faded red roofs nestled behind white picket fences. No two homes were on the same level. Wisps of cloud as cool and damp as Nan-

tucket fog blew past, muting the colors of flowers and occasionally blotting out the distant glint of the sea.

Driving on, we arrived at Windwardside, where Win Parks awaited us at the guesthouse. There we watched sunset colors tint sea and cloud far below our aerie. We seemed part of a never-never land that somehow had come true.

Each hour from seven in the morning until nine at night, a man emerged from the combination post office and police station to strike a bell announcing the hour to people in the fields. Each night at six the electric lights we had seen from Statia came on, to be extinguished at eleven after a warning blink.

Islanders and Dutch are working together to gear Saba to the present. "The airport and roads were planned by the Sabians and financed by the Netherlands Government to develop tourism," Gerard van der Wal, the Administrator, told me. "Traditionally the men have had to leave to find work. But now there are fewer opportunities in the merchant marine or in the oil refineries of Aruba and Curaçao. We seek something that will provide employment."

I asked Mr. van der Wal about the roads. When I visited the islands in 1947, the link between Fort Bay landing and The Bottom had just been completed, and children screamed on their first motor trip because the houses went by so fast. "Now we have

A short flight by Dornier 28 (right) and a very crooked road carry visitors from St. Maarten to Windwardside with speed, comfort—and thrills. Sabians designed and built the tortuous track.

Roaring surf pummels nimble boatmen landing cargo at Fort Bay, Saba. For centuries, both freight and fear-numbed passengers reached the isolated island only by this "port of entry." Now visitors land on an airstrip islanders carved from the spur of a mountain.

NATIONAL GEOGRAPHIC PHOTOGRAPHER WINFIELD PARKS

over six miles of paved road, and 50 vehicles, mostly jeeps," said Mr. van der Wal.

"Although engineers from the Netherlands designed the landing field, the roads are native. Lambert Hassell, a Sabian with only elementary schooling, laid them out by walking the terrain and planting stakes. The surfacing was done by manpower—not concrete mixers and bulldozers. Perhaps if he had taken courses in engineering he would have sat at a desk with a slide rule and said, 'Impossible!'"

Motoring down to the landing, I found that steep offshore contours and battering seas still defy construction of a harbor. Every item of food and merchandise brought to Saba must still land through the surf in small boats. While I watched, a crew skidded a boat down the boulder-strewn beach to the water's edge, responding to a signal from a local sloop. After waiting for a lull the crew shoved hard and scrambled aboard, paddling furiously to avoid being overturned by the next crest.

Returning with two women picked up from the sloop, the boatmen had less success. Instead of shooting onto the beach, the bow touched and the boat swung broadside. The following wave broke aboard, soaking the occupants. As the two women struggled up the beach, shoes squishing and suitcases dripping, my driver took it as a joke. "They thinks they has it bad!" he chortled. "But you should watch when it's really rough—and they's landing a jeep!"

"How can they do it?" I asked.

"They ties two boats together, and puts a platform on them. Then they drops an

Like an ogre's fastness, fog-shrouded volcanic cliffs rise behind the dollhouse hamlet of Upper Hell's Gate. Scrubbing diligently, repainting often, villagers keep their homes bright with white walls, green trim, and red roofs.

anchor offshore, and brings two lines ashore. They watches. After they see five, six or seven big seas come in, they generally gets c-a-a-lm. Then they moves in to where planks can reach to the beach, and the jeep drives ashore. But sometimes they can't make it, and the ship has to take the jeep back to St. Maarten, maybe two—three time, waiting for smoother water."

I often wondered why the inhabitants of one of the flattest countries of Europe chose almost the steepest island of the Caribbean for a new homeland. Dutch settlers arrived about 1640, and though the island changed hands among the English, French, and Dutch 12 times, it finally returned to the Dutch on February 21, 1816.

In the early days, vertical slopes were useful for defense. The traveling priest Père Labat, who visited the island in 1701, recounted that in 1688 a French filibuster captain, M. Pinel, was driven off when the Sabians rolled boulders down from wooden stages they had built on the slopes. Again in 1690 a cruising French frigate was repulsed by a similar hail of stones.

An indication of how Sabians have remained isolated through the centuries is the incidence of two family names. "As far back as you can look in the records you will find the name Johnson," Mr. van der Wal said, "and as early as 1677 a James Hassell was mentioned as Vice Commander. In our present population of 1,030, we have 125 Johnsons and 249 Hassells."

During the period when many Saba men went to sea as merchant seamen and officers, most kept a sentimental attachment

Retired sailor Henry Hassell, 89, takes his ease at home on Saba. Watching dancers and singing as he plays, a banjoist strums out a spirited beat.

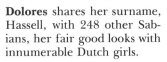

Dolores shares her surname, Hassell, with 248 other Sabians, her fair good looks with innumerable Dutch girls.

for their tiny homeland. Many men returned to marry their childhood sweethearts, sometimes even bringing back with them the timber needed to build a home. Never had I seen cottages which were such visible expressions of love and pride as some of those in Windwardside and the neighboring settlements. Many of the older houses had private burial grounds in their minuscule front yards, as though the inhabitants were loath to leave even in death.

One day after wandering the paths of Upper Hell's Gate, a village even higher up the mountain than Windwardside, Win and I were invited into the house of Mrs. Myrtle Johnson. We began a conversation when she came out to hang some washing from a line behind her cottage. The clothes flapped in the breeze and dangled over a cliff that dropped almost sheer a thousand feet to the airport.

As we talked, I could restrain my curiosity no longer, and asked Mrs. Johnson if she would mind showing us her home. Shyly she led us inside a dwelling that came as close to being a doll's house as a habitation for adults can be.

The first thing to catch my eye in the tiny living room was the phrase "Home Sweet Home," lovingly framed. Flowers were in vases on small tables. The walls were pale blue, hung with two hunting scenes, one a stag in northern woods. A bright pillow from Curaçao adorned the single rocking chair. Flowered curtains matched a flowered oilcloth on the dining table. Never had I seen a house so visibly scrubbed and dusted, yet equally gay and cheerful.

"The bedroom is my daughter Phyllis's," explained Mrs. Johnson, showing us a pale pink chamber. "She is being married soon. My son is a mason who also does carpenter work. He's building a house for her next door." We could see son Franklin hoisting stones into place on a plot that seemed only the size of a billiard table.

"Many Saba houses begin with few rooms when a couple is married," Mrs. Johnson said, "and other rooms are added when the children come." It seemed to me that Phyllis and her husband would need sky hooks to add rooms to their house, as it already hung over the edge.

In the old tradition of Saba women, Mrs. Johnson earned some of her housekeeping money by making dainty handkerchiefs

Capt. Reuben Simmons, formerly of the Holland-America Line, lives in retirement. His door with stained-glass panels represents his own taste; his career at sea, followed by serene years on Saba, the pattern of life for many men of the island.

"Now, pull out another thread . . ." A Sabian artist explains her traditional craft of drawn work to a visitor, who admires an unfinished blouse of so-called "Saba lace" or "Spanish work."

and tablecloths. "People sometimes speak of Saba 'lacework,'" she told us as we examined some exquisitely delicate napkins, "but it is drawn work. See—we pull the threads of the material to get the patterns." It is slow work. Mrs. Johnson's output is only two handkerchiefs a day.

The slightly topsy-turvy quality of Saba extends to its place names. Although Dutch is taught in the schools and is the language used in official documents, English is universally spoken even in the homes. Occasionally this causes confusion. In the town of The Bottom, *Kerkstraat* is painted on the signs, but a stranger asking guidance will be directed to Church Street.

For that matter, naming a town The Bottom when it lies in a bowl-shaped valley some 700 feet above the sea seems illogical by most standards. No doubt English travelers misunderstood *botte*, a word of Dutch derivation meaning "bowl," and interpreted it as "bottom." However, it was "unanimously resolved" at a public meeting of the inhabitants in 1868 to change the name of The Bottom to the town of Leverock "in token of our Love and Esteem for our most worthy and Excellent Lieutenant Gover-

nor." Apparently the resolution was forgotten. Efforts to change the name of Hell's Gate—origin unknown—to Zion's Hill likewise met with no success. The Sabian was long content with things as his forebears had known them.

Yet there are signs that this is changing. Mr. van der Wal told me that "more Sabians live abroad than in Saba."

Miss Julia Crane, from Mount Kisco, New York, was spending a year among the people doing research for a doctorate in anthropology. She told why Saba has sometimes been called the island of women.

Saba acquired this reputation in the late 1930's. The men left to go to sea, sending money back to their wives. Many served as officers, mates, and engineers. Some settled with their families in New York. When maritime jobs grew scarce, Sabians shifted to the oil refineries of Aruba and Curaçao. The women have gone to join them there, and some have found work too. So while other parts of the world have experienced a population explosion, Saba's population has declined.

I was amused to discover that Miss Crane had fallen into the island way of thinking;

as we talked she saw Win Parks passing in the distance, and exclaimed with unconscious curiosity, "Look, another stranger!"

Gazing up at the crags as we had sailed by in *Finisterre,* Henry Davis had commented, "I don't see how you could grow anything there but mountain goats!" Yet the early colonists managed to grow some sugar cane, usually a flat-country crop.

One morning, I started from Windwardside up the slope of the peak above, where I heard that vegetable and fruit gardens grew. I had not gone far before encountering the conditions that the manager of the Windwardside Guesthouse had described to me: "The path is always slippery, walking up, and under the cloud cover it's like it's always raining."

Plodding along, at first in hot sunshine, I suddenly was swallowed in cold mist. Water dripped from every leaf. Even the sounds from the village were muted. I did not reach the top. Sliding backward 11 inches for every foot of progress, I gave up. But I visited there too soon. I learned later from friends that construction had started on a step road to permit walking up to the peak.

Despite its venture into the 20th century, Saba remains aloof. "We have not more than 200 overnight visitors a year," Mr. van der Wal told me on our last day, when we were waiting for the plane at the airport. "Most tourists come over for the few hours between planes on the days when we have morning and evening flights. You can hardly call us overrun."

On take-off we were over the sea the moment our wheels left the runway. I had a brief glimpse of waves crashing on rocks below; then we climbed steeply. The road wound up Saba's slope like a design in spun sugar. Hell's Gate seen from above reminded me of an Italian hill town — a cluster of houses around a stone church, perched atop a green peak. We skimmed the rooftops of Windwardside, looked down into The Bottom, and straightened out for St. Maarten. I twisted in my seat to look back at Saba, once more diminished to a cone

Passengers from the Holland-America Line's *Maasdam,* moored at Point Blanche on St. Maarten, choose luxury goods at free-port prices in Philipsburg. Gable-high "B" on the Courthouse honors a royal visitor — Crown Princess Beatrix, heiress to the throne of the Netherlands.

rising from the sea; even on renewed acquaintance it remained shrouded in mist, mystery, and otherworldliness.

St. Maarten brought us back to the present with a jolt. Taxis waited in a line behind a glass-fronted airport terminal. "Dinner for four?" repeated the maître d'hôtel of a smart restaurant in Philipsburg. "Sorry. We're booked up. Reservations are necessary during the season." St. Maarten was in the midst of a boom.

Seldom in such a short time and distance have I visited islands as different as Saba and St. Maarten. Their only common denominator seemed that they are both part of the Netherlands Windward Islands. But not even that applied completely, for the French, since 1648, have shared ownership of the island. Their part is called St. Martin.

There is no visible frontier and little difference in terrain. English is the common language except on official documents, so a stranger may go from the Dutch to the French part without realizing it. However, as most maps use the French spelling for the island as a whole, I will do the same.

Where Saba is all up and down, St. Martin is relatively flat. Where Saba has no harbors and its "beaches" are slopes of stones, St. Martin has dozens of bays, most of them rimmed by chalk-white sand.

*T*HE COMBINATION of bays and beaches not only encourages commerce but also lures visitors to the island. New hotels are going up, but not fast enough. "We are having difficulty keeping up with the demand for rooms," I was told by *Gezaghebber* J. J. Beaujon, the Lieutenant Governor of the Netherlands Windward Islands. "With traffic to the Caribbean increasing each year, we seem to be getting more than our share."

Another reason for the boom is that both St. Maarten and St. Martin are free of import levies. A guidebook explains that there are no guards, no customs inspectors, no language barriers, no exchange problems. The banks will open accounts in any currency, even in troy ounces of fine gold, and it is guaranteed by license that whatever currency is brought in can be taken out in like form. Cash in any currency will pay for merchandise.

The capital of St. Maarten is Philipsburg. It occupies a long, narrow sandspit between the ocean and a salt pond that was once the principal source of island income. At high tide seawater was admitted to flat pens created in the lagoon by stone dikes. After sluice gates were closed, the sun went to work, and in a few months burned away the moisture until only salt crystals remained. Even the Caribs knew Great Salt Pond; the Indian name for the island was Sualouiga, "the Land of Salt."

Now only a few stone walls and floodgates remain, but even these produce a strange beauty. When evaporation occurs and the density of the water increases, red algae appear in the brine. As Win and I walked along the lagoon, we looked at ponds ranging from delicate pink to deep rose, contrasting with the blue Caribbean visible beyond the sandspit of Philipsburg. Along the shore caked salt lay like drifts of snow.

Philipsburg in plan looks like a ladder. Two thoroughfares run the length of the city, forming the uprights, Front Street paralleling the bay and Back Street running along the lagoon. Short cross streets with Dutch names I could hardly pronounce form the rungs. Up and down and across, shops sell merchandise imported from everywhere. In wonder Mel and I walked along Front Street looking at Danish silver, Swiss watches, English porcelain, Swedish crystal, German cameras, French handbags, Japanese radios, Italian shoes, Dutch meerschaum pipes, and Scottish sweaters.

Just as there are no barriers against the outside world, there are none between the political divisions of the island. Driving from Philipsburg to Marigot, capital of French St. Martin, we encountered only a simple marker at the roadside, placed in 1948 to commemorate three centuries of coexistence. One side said Sint Maarten, the other Saint Martin. We passed from the territory of one sovereign nation to another with none of the usual complications.

Like St. Kitts, St. Martin was settled by groups from two rival European nations. As on St. Kitts, bickering began and developed into fighting. But unlike their neighbors, the Dutch and French colonists agreed by treaty to divide the territory in 1648.

Japanese fishermen based on Philipsburg catch yellowfin and albacore tuna and other deep-sea fish off the Dutch Windwards. Frozen fresh, most of the fish go to canneries on Puerto Rico.

"*Le Blanc* is winning!" Fighting cocks clash in a blur of feathers and blood—a spectator sport at Marigot, capital of the French side of St. Martin. Before pitting his bird, the owner clips its wings and fastens the gaffs—long, razor-sharp steel blades—to the spurs on its legs.

Legend has it that the division between the two nations was settled by placing a Dutchman and a Frenchman back to back at the water's edge, and telling them to walk around the perimeter till they met. A line between the two points would form a boundary, the French getting everything to the north, the Dutch to the south. The soldiers started out briskly, each carrying a canteen of water, but the Dutchman added a flask of Holland gin on the sly. After a few nips the Dutchman stopped to nap in the shade of a tree while the Frenchman plodded along, covering more distance.

Historians, of course, deny this. The French colony was strengthened by troops sent from St. Kitts. These forced a settlement on March 23, 1648, "by which the island was divided between the two nations, and the equal rights of the inhabitants to the salt-ponds, chase, fishing waters, dyewoods, minerals, harbours and bays of the island recognized." Regardless of how the division was effected, the French got 20 square miles of territory and the Dutch 14.

We found that each part of the island retained its own character. Although Marigot's shops sold almost the same range and variety of merchandise we had seen in Philipsburg, and at comparable prices, I found it had remained much more in the West Indian tradition. While the Dutch seemed tuned to Princess Juliana Airport and the steamers unloading alongside the dock in the Great Bay, the French capital took its pace from local sloops and schooners bringing produce from neighboring Anguilla. Strolling among the vendors in the waterfront market, I was reminded of the leisurely-paced islands to the south.

Perhaps for this reason I was somewhat overwhelmed on returning to Philipsburg. Driving to the extremity of the eastern point forming Great Bay, I found a commercial boom to equal the tourist influx. Tucked into a valley near Point Blanche offices and warehouses stood cheek by jowl in a swirl of dust. But the available space was not enough. Feverishly bulldozers and other earth-moving equipment bit into the hillside, making room for more buildings. Meanwhile mounds of merchandise being unloaded from ships were piled along the road and covered with tarpaulins, for lack of warehouse space.

Walking along the modern concrete dock, large enough to accommodate several freighters at once, I came on a group of vessels flying the flag of Japan. Cargo winches rattled as they lifted clusters of frozen tuna from small craft resembling whaleship chasers. Slung by a loop around their tails, the fish dangled like huge bunches of bananas.

Crewmen climbed from the frigid interior into the blazing sunshine, wearing heavy coats, fur caps, mittens, and thick insulated boots. Ton after ton disappeared into the refrigerated holds of *Chikuzen,* a mother ship. Hearing shouted orders, I felt I might have been on the dock at Misaki, the fishing port which supplies Tokyo. Forming a frieze along the upper rails of the boats were hundreds of drying sharks' fins and tails, used to make Chinese soup.

Amazingly, we had found a shortage of fish everywhere we had been. A stranger might assume that the converging Atlantic and Caribbean waters would teem with fish. Yet they were rare in local markets. In communities all along our route a knot of women would congregate on the beach whenever a canoe headed toward shore,

173

hoping there would be a catch for sale.

The reason for the scarcity, I felt, was that the narrow band of shallows fringing the islands had been largely depleted of reef dwellers through the years, while trade-wind seas made it difficult for the fragile gommiers to seek the pelagic varieties.

Now the Japanese, fishing far off shore, use modern methods to reap a finned harvest. Fishing boats and mother ship are studded with electronic gear: Echo sounders reveal schools far below the surface and radio calls other ships to the area of a heavy run. The Japanese tackle could be carried aboard sizable craft only. Decks of the chaser were piled with flagged bamboo poles, miles of line coiled in tubs, and glass floats patterned by woven rope nets.

"We built a freezer plant here in June, 1964, and have ten ships operating out of Philipsburg," Hiroshi Shimamori, executive director of Curaçao Pioneering, N. V., told me when I visited him in his office near the dock. Behind his desk an elaborately coiffured and kimonoed geisha doll stood in a black lacquer-and-glass case. Nearby, on a low table, were arranged the cups and saucers of the traditional tea service of Japan.

"We take tuna—both albacore and yellowfin—and tunalike fish: big eye marlin, sailfish, swordfish, kingfish, and dolphin," Mr. Shimamori said. "Only about 5 percent of our catch is shipped to Japan. The majority goes to Puerto Rico for canning. We also sell tunalike fish throughout the Caribbean. Each Monday we sell fish to residents on St. Maarten at very low prices."

Some 30 Japanese fishermen are based on St. Maarten, not counting crews of the trawlers in port. Every three months a ship comes out from Japan to bring supplies and take back a cargo of frozen fish. Those living ashore or aboard *Chikuzen* have their own club near Philipsburg, forming a small outpost of Nippon. When I asked Mr. Shimamori what his compatriots ate, after telling him I shared the Japanese love for raw fish, he smiled. "Ah! Each day we eat well! Especially the *sashimi*, thin slices of tuna dipped in soya, and *sushi*, with balls of rice."

In only one way were we disappointed by Philipsburg. Ever since sailing from English Harbour, *Finisterre* had rolled to swells in open roadsteads. We had rolled when anchored off Nevis, rolled in St. Kitts, rolled in Statia, and now continued to be uncomfortable in swells that curled around Point Blanche. Thus I looked forward to our next port, Gustavia on St. Barthélemy. On the chart it looked perfect, a snug pocket in the land.

No sooner had *Finisterre* rounded the peninsula protecting Philipsburg's bay—called Witte Kaap by the Dutch, Pointe Blanche by the French, and White Cap by the islanders—than we had to flatten sails. On the bay the wind had been fresh, but as we drew away from shore I realized that williwaws of breeze funneling down the slopes had fooled me into carrying too small a jib. *Finisterre* gently rose and fell to the seas, lacking drive. From the snail's pace of the bubbles alongside it was obvious we were getting nowhere. Squinting at them lazily, I hoped no one else would notice.

"Well, skipper?" asked Mel Grosvenor with a rising inflection, mildly protesting our inefficient rig. So I temporarily abandoned sun-bathing to help set a larger jib.

Now *Finisterre* came alive. We sliced through the crests, and foam hissed along the sides. St. Barthélemy lay almost dead in the eye of the wind. One tack took us close to a cluster of rocks lying on the bank of soundings joining the two islands; another, out over the ocean abyss toward Statia and St. Kitts, shadowy on the distant horizon. At 11:45 the ship's log recorded: "Sighted whale breaching clear of water, falling back with geyser of spray."

In the afternoon the wind freshened and the seas became bigger. We drove hard toward Sugarloaf, a detached rock off the St. Barthélemy coast, that divides the approach to Gustavia into two channels. As we came on soundings, the crests grew higher. *Finisterre* plunged through until we were close under a lighthouse standing on a bluff. As I struggled to muzzle the genoa, I looked over my shoulder at the entrance to the harbor. "Peace," I thought, "it's going to be wonderful!"

Lazy afternoon at Marigot Bay: A single fisherman pulls his boat into deeper water. Starting the outboard and chugging away, he will dodge unmarked shoals in the western harbor.

XII   *St. Barts:*
Memories of Sweden

Tiny Gustavia's pocket port dips into the edge of St. Barts. A shopping center for the Caribbea

A s we powered through the narrow entrance, sails furled, Gustavia appeared over the bow as the embodiment of tranquillity, a little village somnolent in the sunshine of a Sunday afternoon. The hillside above the shuttered houses was empty. The decks of the few island trading vessels around the rim of the harbor were deserted. Flags drooped and the water lay flat. It was just as I had expected.

Alas! We had no sooner made fast to a dock we did not realize was private than we were ousted by a vociferous boatman. On transferring to a nearby stone quay, we found that the placidity of the harbor was only an illusion.

After we dropped anchor and hauled *Finisterre*'s stern to the shore, a practically invisible surge sent us shooting ahead and astern, fetching up against our lines with an impact that almost brought us to our knees. Long, low swells curled around the protecting point of land. As each rolled in, *Finisterre* went ahead with it; when it receded, she surged back until checked by the anchor—a restless dance that was to go on through the night.

We were still wondering whether the lines would hold when a new disturbance startled us. A din sounded from the far side of the harbor—a cacophony of blaring horns and loud singing. Looking across, we saw a cavalcade of automobiles and trucks surging over the crest of the hillside behind the town. As we watched, the noise doubled, for a second parade of vehicles

e duty-free town sells a variety of wares for less than they cost in the countries that produce them.

began winding up the road from town. When the two met, shouted slogans combined with the singing and blast of horns. We had arrived on election eve and the rival political factions were whooping it up before voting for a mayor.

Despite our jarring welcome, St. Barts—a contraction of St. Barthélemy—remains in my memory as one of the most charming islands of our cruise. Stone fences, remnants of planter days, pattern the hillsides, tokens of intensive cultivation. Campeche and tamarind trees abound. Islanders use campeche for dyewood; processed tamarind goes into beverages popular throughout the islands.

Gustavia added a dash of Scandinavia to the smorgasbord of cultures we already had encountered. In 1784 France ceded St. Barts to Sweden in exchange for the right to establish a transshipment center at Göteborg. For almost a century the island remained an outpost of Sweden, far from the skerries of the Baltic.

Remnants of a coaling station and a hospital of imported yellow brick stand opposite Gustavia, named for the Swedish king, Gustavus III. Although the island was sold back to France in 1877, traces of northern influence remain in the small windows and scrollwork on many houses. Towheaded children, who would look at home in Sweden, are actually descendants of the original Norman and Breton settlers.

A smaller version of St. Martin, St. Barts also has no customs duties, and I stocked *Finisterre* at bargain rates for our passage to the Virgin Islands. Prices seemed lower at Gustavia than at any other port we visited. We found canned French delicacies and wines selling for prices hard to believe, and at a dockside store I bought Barbados rum at 80 cents a bottle—less than I had paid for the same brand on the British island where it was made.

Like a smaller version of St. Martin, too, St. Barts has a scalloped shoreline, deeply indented bays cradling beautiful white sand beaches. To reach those on the northern shore we hired a car.

Time stands still for children at play beside a Swedish clock tower. Long ago, a large bell within sounded an alarm when fire broke out.

Fair skin of the people of St. Barts reflects Norman and Breton ancestry, while bare feet and warm smiles hint at a carefree life. A basket weaver carries on traditions of the past century, and frilled bonnets recall the dress of early French settlers.

FRED WARD, BLACK STAR

179

Gustavian voters revel with loud singing and blaring horns before choosing a mayor. The author arrived at the usually sleepy port on election eve. His yawl and Boston Whaler bob at the quay.

Gourmet's delight, huge clawless lobsters emerge from a tidal pool. *Finisterre*'s crew boiled the langoustes in water scooped from the sea. Pensive eyes mask the dreams of an island girl (left).

We had barely climbed to the top of the hill behind Gustavia when a small airplane seemed to be diving into our window.

"Duck!" Mel exclaimed involuntarily.

Because the landing strip lies in the valley beyond, one of the few flat spots on the island, a pilot must cut his power where the road crosses the crest, then follow the slope of the hillside down to the field.

Soon we came to the Eden Rock Guest House, perched on a jutting promontory with beaches on both sides. From the balcony in front we had a spectacular view of a coral reef below, with every detail visible through the clear water. While Win Parks took pictures and I jotted in my notebook, Mel Grosvenor disappeared. When he came back he was smiling. "Follow me," he said, "and I'll show you dinner."

Under the guesthouse was a rock-walled pool open to the tide. There Mel pointed to dozens of langoustes, the clawless lobsters of tropical waters, penned for diners' choice. From every shaded cavern long antennae protruded, and other fine specimens crawled across the sandy bottom. Two small boys stood by to catch those wanted. "We'll take that one, and that, and that," said Mel, choosing sizes to fit *Finisterre*'s biggest cooking pot.

Shortly after our arrival on St. Barts, we met M. and Mme Henri Pitany of Paris, who had sailed across from France in a small yacht with their nine-year-old son as crew. The Pitanys had helped us moor, and we had invited them aboard for an apéritif before dinner.

The Pitanys regarded their small cruiser as a home away from home. We had met similar couples of other nationalities on our way through the islands. Finding a harbor they liked, they would settle for a while, soaking up sunshine and living inexpensively, and when the mood dictated they would move on, almost as free as the wind that bore them.

Now on their way to the Virgin Islands and their ultimate goal, Nassau, the Pitanys were in no hurry to leave St. Barts. *Le petit* was learning to swim and dive for shells, and *papa* and *maman* were equally content in this tiny tropical bit of France. "*C'est une île très charmante*," M. Pitany told me, and went on to say that the surge was most unusual, that normally the water of the harbor was *calme plat*.

Before leaving we visited the winter residence of banker David Rockefeller of New York. Nelson W. Aldrich, the architect who designed the house and supervised its construction, invited us to inspect this unique home, built on an isolated point that can be reached only by boat.

"The house took a year and a half on the drawing board," Mr. Aldrich told me as we walked through rooms of unorthodox shape, "and it was four years building. The basis is a parabola, a shape similar to an ellipse except that the lines never meet—it is as free a mathematical curve as can be achieved. We chose the form partially to funnel the breezes through, taking advantage of nature's air conditioning."

FROM A TERRACE which curved around the front of the living-room area, we enjoyed a magnificent view, blue water on two sides dotted by small islands and off-lying rocks. The house seemed to be a continuation of the hillside, its contours and texture blending into its surroundings.

Nearby was a smaller building, completely different in form. "The detached guesthouse is triangular, to get as far away in design from the main house as possible," Mr. Aldrich continued, "but also to pick up the feel of the conical rocks and the triangular shape of beacons and buoys, as it is oriented to the sea."

Later that afternoon, sailing for the Anegada Passage, I took a bearing from the cockpit of *Finisterre* on the triangular house as easily as on any beacon, crossing it with the lighthouse above Gustavia. To starboard lay a collection of dangers to be avoided, a scattering of pinnacles rising abruptly from deep water—islets with the unromantic names of Beef Barrel, Big and Little Groupers, and Hen and Chickens, where it would be even more unromantic to stage a shipwreck.

Slowly we moved out into the Anegada Passage, our longest open-ocean run of the cruise—just under 100 miles from Gustavia to Round Rock, in the Virgin Islands. Under the hills of St. Barts the breeze was light and baffling, but as we cleared the land the trade wind came in from astern, still light in force.

Lifting gently to a succession of small swells which slid under the stern, *Finisterre* rolled over the darkening sea. The sky was cloudless, and when the sun dropped below the horizon stars shone immediately brilliant in the violet afterglow.

At 1945 hours ship's time—7:45 p.m. ashore—I entered in the log: "Wind east-southeast, moderate. Sky clear, sea slight. Lights of Philipsburg abeam. Now clear all dangers until the Virgin Islands."

Quietly under our canopy of stars we slipped through the night, the only sound the splash of the bow wave and the occasional creak of the main boom. At the end of its long painter, the Boston Whaler still followed along behind like a faithful dog. On the eight o'clock change of watch, Henry called us below to a dinner of Mel's langoustes, boiled in seawater scooped from over the side.

To gourmets who think the lobster of northern latitudes beyond compare, I recommend langouste cooked in naturally salted water until tender—but no longer—served with melted butter, the juice of small green limes, and crushed red peppers.

Afterward Mel took the wheel while I sat near him in the cockpit. Our watch

system was informal: two six-hour day tricks, splitting the hours from seven in the morning until seven at night, and three four-hour watches through the darkness. In planning *Finisterre* for cruising as well as racing, I had arranged lines for trimming sails within reach of the helmsman so that only one man need be on deck in fair weather. Therefore when our conversation waned, as the warm breeze and gentle motion lulled me, I sought my bunk, leaving Mel alone with his thoughts and the stars.

When I came back on deck, conditions were unchanged except that the wind had gone more directly astern. Working together, we clipped the jib to a spinnaker pole and pushed it out on the side opposite the main boom. Oldtime sailors referred to this procedure picturesquely as running "wing and wing." Now it was Mel's turn to bid me a sleepy good night.

Even after years of sailing there is something fascinating to me about a small boat on the sea at night—a unique sense of detachment, as though the rest of the world no longer existed. The mast wove a pattern among the stars, the breeze was warm and friendly on my bare shoulders, and the lift of *Finisterre* to the seas was a lullaby.

With dawn the purple shapes of the Virgins archipelago showed on the horizon. When Columbus found the same cluster of peaks, they seemed so numerous they reminded him of the legend of St. Ursula and the Eleven Thousand Virgins.

Ursula was a princess who begged her father to allow her to go on a cruise to avoid becoming the wife of a pagan king. She invited ten maidens to accompany her; but others implored her to include them. When she finally sailed, it took 11 ships of her father's navy to transport the 11,000 young ladies who had signed on.

For three years they roamed the seas. On the day they disembarked at Cologne, the Huns sacked the city, slaying Ursula and all her companions. Columbus immortalized the maidens when he named the archipelago *Las Vírgenes* in their honor.

Exploring the shallows, a finned swimmer snorkels near a reef off St. Barts. Eden Rock Guest House (right) caps a promontory of the rocky isle. In the wide bays that sweep far inland, crescents of white sand embrace pale blue waters.

XIII *The Virgin Islands:*
Gems in a Pirate Sea

In Deadman Bay, *Finisterre* floats above her own shadow as crew members on Peter Island scrub tl

As *Finisterre* came on soundings in the Round Rock Passage, islands stretched away on either beam. To starboard the ample contours of Virgin Gorda, the "Fat Virgin," rose above a fringe of lesser cays, while to port others lay on the velvet sea like jewels scattered by a careless pirate: Ginger and Carval Rock, Cooper and Salt, Dead Chest and Peter.

Columbus had dispatched a force of caravels through the same opening by which we entered, and they had reported "a main large sea having in it innumerable islands, marvellously differing one from another." But the "main large sea," in reality a wide lane of deep water between the Atlantic and the Caribbean, takes its name from someone else. For me it is a unique channel, best described by the *New Sailing Directions for the Caribbee Islands* — the yellowed, brittle pages of the edition of 1818: "Happily ... nature has arranged [the islands] as to form a grand basin, in the midst, wherein ships may lie at anchor, land-locked, and sheltered from every wind. This basin, or harbour, is the finest that can be imagined, and is called Sir Francis Drake's Bay or Channel; it having been entered by that commander in 1580 [1585], when he proceeded against St. Domingo."

Whaler. Beyond a pipe-organ cactus rises Tortola. Pirates gave palisaded Dead Chest Cay its name.

The administrative center of the British Virgin Islands is Roadtown, on Tortola Island. We were supposed to enter there, but since it was almost time for lunch, and I remembered a cove near the tip of Virgin Gorda that was a lovely spot to anchor, we made our way back toward the east, paralleling a weird formation.

A strange freak of nature had dumped huge squarish boulders on a low cay, then tumbled them about. It had reminded some unknown early navigator of a ruined city, and so remains on most charts to this day as Fallen Jerusalem.

Henry dropped the anchor overside, and we watched it plummet through the clear water, leaving a trail of silver bubbles. Soon we followed for a swim and then set the table for lunch in the cockpit. Afterward, before making for Roadtown, came a siesta, of course.

Roadtown had changed. I had first known it as a tiny settlement, with vegetable plots on the hillsides and a fleet of fishing sloops anchored off a concrete dock. Now diesel ferries to St. John and St. Thomas, in United States territory, bustled in and out. Taxis painted in gaudy colors waited at the head of the wharf. The Detroit-built station wagons looked as long as Pullman cars after the small European automobiles of the southern islands.

When I tried to pay my taxi driver in the currency of the British West Indies, he stared at it curiously. "What's that?" he demanded. "We takes only U. S. dollars here." Economically, the British Virgin Islands are almost completely oriented to their American cousins.

Shortly before we arrived, President Lyndon B. Johnson had declared the U. S. Virgin Islands a disaster area. Ever since leaving Dominica, with its "pipeline to the sky," we had watched the islands become progressively more sere. Now the British Virgins, too, were burned brown, victims

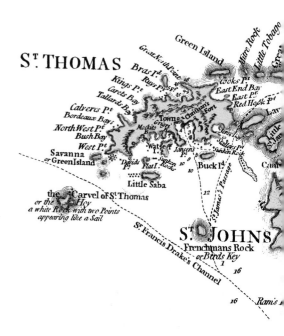

Notorious haunt of Caribbean freebooters, the Virgin Islands sprinkle an English map of 1797. Pirates — like those intent on a division of booty in Howard Pyle's painting — found refuge among the maze of cays and hidden inlets. Today Britain administers most of the group northeast of old St. Johns, and the United States supervises the islands to the west and south.

ANEGADA *or* Drowned Island
almost entirely cover'd by the Sea
at spring tides

Freebooters
Point

Mangroves

Low and flat Ground

Mangroves

Treasure Point
so called by ye Freebooters from the
Gold & Silver supposed to have
been bury'd there abouts
after the Wreck of a Spanish Galleon

2 feet

Dangerous

2 feet Reef

6 feet

Horse Shu

Little Van Dykes

Green
Island

Cammanoes Island

Fishermans Head

Guana I.

Scrubb Island

Dog Keys

Sunken Rock

Dog Isl.

St Francis Drake's Channel

Moskito I.

Nicker I.

Sunken Rock

Prickly Pear

West Bay

the Sound

East Bay

Flat Cove

TOLA

Brewers Bay

Little Garden

Road

Town Fort

Pot Hog Bay

Harbour Road

Seatons Bay

Beef I.

Fort

South Bay

East End

VIRGIN GORDA or
SPANISH TOWN

Dutch Head

Frenchmans Key

the Virgins Gangway of the Freebooters

Sr FRANCIS DRAKE'S BAY
who first sailed through these Islands in 1580
and found the Depth from 10 to 25 fathom
very rocky

Salt I.

Broken Islands
and Rocks
called
the Fallen City *or*
Old Jerusalem

Round Rock

North
Fort

English Keys

Peters
Island

Witch

Ducks I.

Fort

the Dead Chest

Ginger Island

Coopers Island

the King's Channel

W.Pt

Normands Island

of man's greed and carelessness. Once the entire Virgin Islands group was verdant. Trees grew to the water's edge, but careless timbering and planting by early settlers caused cumulative erosion until many of the islands turned into virtual deserts of scrub-covered rock.

We had heard, however, of a rain forest carefully preserved on the slopes of Mt. Sage, and Mel hired a Land-Rover so we could have a look. As we neared the cooler upper slopes, green shoots broke through the crusted earth, patterned by darker streaks that followed ravines holding moisture after a shower.

On the highest peaks of Mt. Sage, we arrived at an area where the trees had not been cut. The difference became immediately apparent. Undergrowth sprouted and the unfamiliar smell of damp soil filled the air. Though this was no rain forest comparable to the impenetrable growths we had seen on some southern islands, it was nevertheless a demonstration of the ability of wooded peaks to draw moisture from the atmosphere.

The forest was part of Laurance S. Rockefeller's program. It is impossible to write about the Virgins archipelago without paying tribute to the vision of this American

FRED WARD, BLACK STAR

Queen Elizabeth II and Prince Philip greet officials on Tortola during their Caribbean tour in 1966. Britain's royal couple flanks Superintendent of Agriculture J. L. M. Winter. To honor their sovereign, the islanders named a new bridge after her.

A hero's channel — Sir Francis Drake's — sweeps past Tortola. From the capital of Roadtown, below Mount Manuel, Her Majesty's representatives govern the British Virgin Islands.

philanthropist. Not only on Virgin Gorda but also on St. John he has bought land for future generations to enjoy. He donated holdings on St. John for the new Virgin Islands National Park.

O N OUR WAY BACK to Roadtown we looked down on a terraced hillside and saw sugar cane being cut, loaded on donkeys, and carried to a small mill. Intrigued, Mel Grosvenor suggested we find out what was going on. We left the Land-Rover and plunged down a steep path to a small agricultural-industrial complex in a clearing. To the swish of knives and the voices of the cutters in the nearby field, the stalks were taken off the backs of the donkeys and fed directly between iron rollers. The juice — pure "cane squeezin's" — ran down a concrete trough to a still.

Dubiously we approached, fearing that the hissing still might blow up at any moment. Pieces of rope held together a serpentine coil. Wisps of vapor escaped, and from the bottom of the coil a clear stream flowed from a spigot.

Mel leaned closer to have a look at the crude contraption and was handed a brimming calabash of rum, warm and reeking, right from the still. After one sniff he

Palm fronds feather a pool on Virgin Gorda Island, where sun-seeking families wade still wate

recoiled, exclaiming, "Now I know what Ozark 'white lightning' must be like!"

On returning from the highland, we hove in the anchor and hoisted sails at sunset to go reaching across Sir Francis Drake Channel. One of the things so fascinating about Virgin Islands cruising is that around the next headland from a settlement is always a deserted anchorage.

Within minutes we dropped anchor again, this time in Deadman Bay on Peter Island, the kind of setting a man might dream about when sleet rattles against the windowpane. A patchwork of pale green and blue shallows lay embraced by a semicircle of white sand, backed by towering coconut palms. Conning our way in by watching the bottom through the limpid water, we came to rest in the center.

Our nearest neighbor was a bleak little cay named Dead Chest. There, tradition holds, the pirate Blackbeard marooned a mutinous crew, inspiring Robert Louis

Stevenson's famous chant in *Treasure Island:*
Fifteen men on the dead man's chest—
Yo-ho-ho, and a bottle of rum!

Next morning we turned to, much as pirates might have done before a foray. We made fast a line to a palm tree and hauled *Finisterre*'s bow to the beach. Standing in the shallows, we scrubbed away marine growth that had accumulated on the hull. Then we gave the same treatment to the Whaler, resulting in such improved performance that I could not resist a long session of water-skiing.

IN THE AFTERNOON, leaving *Finisterre* tied to her palm, we sped to Dead Chest in the Whaler to snorkel among the offlying reefs. One huge coral formation that thrust from the depths reminded me of the thick gnarled trunk and spreading branches of an apple tree. So vivid was the illusion that after diving I was almost surprised to come up empty-handed.

walled from Spring Bay by massive granite boulders.

Rocks three stories high seclude beachcombers gathering shells in The Baths on Virgin Gorda —a labyrinth sculptured by wind and wave.

Our perfect day faded through the colors of a tropic sunset into silvery brilliance as a bright moon lighted the sea. The sand beach, in the words of Mel Grosvenor, "gleamed exactly like a snowbank," and details on the bottom were almost as clear as by the light of day.

While Mel, Win, and I listened to music in the cockpit, Henry was busy in the galley preparing the crowning touch: succulent steamed conch, an island delicacy he had learned to cook years before when we cruised the Bahamas.

Morning brought a beat back to windward, toward our next goal, Laurance Rockefeller's development at Little Dix Bay on Virgin Gorda. There we found a concrete dock and buoys put down for visiting yachts. On going ashore, we saw a sign in a trim building that invited us to pick up a telephone and make our wants known to the management. Within minutes a jeep arrived to take us to the hotel. Going over a crest, we looked down at a complex of buildings, a central restaurant-lounge surrounded by cottages tucked among the palms, all facing a bay of breathtaking beauty.

Only later did I appreciate the vastness of the project. To place such a modern hotel on a remote and primitive island is quite an engineering feat. "We distill 16,000 gallons of fresh water a day from the sea," Fred Rhodes, the maintenance superintendent, told me proudly. "Our electrical output is enough for a smallish city. We have deep freezes that are really refrigerated warehouses, and a laundry, and our own machine shops."

Work started on the resort in 1961, and

191

Wave-battered bow of the freighter
Rocas juts from waters off Anegada
Island. More than three decades ago
her hull ripped open on deadly Horse
Shoe Reef, a knife-edged coral barrier
that arcs 13 miles along a main gateway between the Atlantic and the Caribbean. Over the centuries, the reef
has sent scores of ships to the bottom.
Finisterre's crew, equipped with snorkels, explored the *Rocas* and found its
macabre cargo—animal bones bound
for a fertilizer factory. The author sur-
faces with a coral-encrusted cannon ball
that went down with a British frigate
in the late 18th or early 19th century.

it opened in January, 1964. Problems of getting a staff on an island with a population of 600, few of whom had ever seen a tablecloth or stem glassware, led to an extensive program for training islanders as waiters, janitors, and chambermaids.

Part of the charm of Little Dix Bay is its location on a beach protected by a coral reef with only a single narrow opening. The lagoon inside invites lazy swimming in almost any weather. But not far away lie less friendly coral formations, part of the deadly trap of the Anegada Passage.

On our second morning we roared out through North Sound by fast motorboat to explore one of the most dangerous graveyards of ships, the reef lying between the tips of Anegada Island and Virgin Gorda. Our pilot was Paul West, a former U. S. Navy submariner who now operates a charter service.

"Horse Shoe Reef is more than ten miles long," Paul told me. "It rises above the surface in only a few places. A giant washboard of ridges and valleys, some ten fathoms deep, it abounds with fish. Staghorn and other coral formations grow on the slopes, along with sea fans, in every brilliant color you can imagine. But Horse Shoe Reef is as dangerous as it is beautiful. During darkness or in bad weather it would be invisible until a ship was in the breakers. More than 300 vessels have left their bones here."

Except for the pale color of the water, the place where we anchored seemed to be open ocean. Putting on swim fins and a face mask, I followed Paul over the side. I felt as though I were floating on the ceiling of a strange and wondrous room. Looking down, I saw a fairy garden filled with colors and forms of infinite variety. Suddenly Paul swam into view. Turning on his side, he pointed to something below.

Strewn across an open patch of sand, surrounded by sea fans and coral, were unmistakable outlines of muzzle-loading cannon. I followed Paul down and he pointed to gun markings he had cleaned on a previous visit, the broad arrow of British naval ordnance. He told me later that research had established the wreck as most probably a frigate of the late 18th or early 19th century. Between the crisscrossed guns were scattered round objects which I recognized as cannon balls even through their growths of coral. Lungs aching for

Peaked roofs of the dining pavilion at Little Dix Bay resort lift above *Finisterre*, anchored in rhinestone waters off Virgin Gorda Island. Laurance S. Rockefeller, a Trustee of the National Geographic Society, opened the retreat in 1964, giving new life to the island's economy.

Skipper checks the centerboard for marine growth. The bronze fin lessens drift when the yawl works to windward.

Fruit of the sea delights a young couple sampling conch salad and lobster prepared by a Swiss chef at Little Dix Bay. The day's menu arrived fresh from waters off the island.

Awash in an agate bay, a visitor to the resort lazes on a water wing. Horseback riding, hiking, fishing, and a simple quest for quiet lure guests to the island.

195

Set aglow by the last rays of evening, *Finisterre* glides on a golden sea past the slender snout of th

air, I made a final lunge to seize the nearest and managed to get it to the surface.

Only a few hundred yards away lay another wreck. "This is a real spooky one," Paul said, grinning but refusing to tell me why. "It's a freighter named *Rocas;* islanders say she was driven ashore during a storm in 1929. Each time I see it I feel like a kid in a haunted house."

We dropped anchor near what seemed one of the few pinnacles of reef above the surface, and Mel, Paul, and I slipped into the water. We hung suspended above a large iron ship. At first glance *Rocas* seemed almost intact. I could see chain, winches, even cargo booms. But then I realized I could also see her boilers and an engine,

standing upright as though ready to continue the voyage—a weird X-ray view of a ship. I could see, too, that what I had thought a pinnacle of reef was actually the stem of the ship, hanging on a ledge. *Rocas* sloped downward till the stern was submerged some ten fathoms.

Then I saw what made *Rocas* a spooky wreck. Around her shattered sides, bones carpeted the sea floor—thousands of bones. Seeing huge jaws and teeth, I realized they were of horses and not of humans, but nevertheless my imagination sped to the sharks that such a cargo would attract.

I envisioned the scene: the *Rocas* striking the reef, passengers and crew abandoning ship, the horses whinnying in terror as they

iguana-shaped rock that gave Guana Island its name.

phosphates, not living animals. Otherwise, nothing would remain." Even with this explanation the spooky feeling persisted.

Curious about Paul's anti-shark yell, I asked him to tell me more. "I don't know why, but it works," he said seriously. "Sharks tend to circle a swimmer, but if they head in I give a shrill short piercing yell and charge. They always turn. Generally they come back—sometimes three or four times —but each time they turn when I charge them yelling. Meanwhile, I'm getting back to the boat as fast as I can."

BACK ASHORE, having encountered no sharks hard of hearing, we found that Virgin Gorda had more than its share of terrestrial oddities. At one time it was famous for copper mines, and bits of bright green ore are still brought up from the abandoned shafts to manufacture simple jewelry, an island handicraft. But perhaps even rarer metals await scientific investigation. Vanceto Waters, a resident of Spanish Town, told me that in 1958 he had worked for a team of geologists, taking samples from the old mines; traces of uranium have been found at a depth of 136 feet.

The geologic formation I will never forget is The Baths of Virgin Gorda, not far from Fallen Jerusalem. Along the shore were piled granite boulders, many larger than two-story houses. Some were pointed like church spires, others were neatly squared; many had curious potholes in their sides. One great circular boulder, balanced atop others like a huge poker chip, had a flat upper surface that attracted sunbathers. All the vast rocks were polished almost smooth.

The most curious thing about these boulders was the way they had been strewn along the white sand beach, much as a child might scatter pebbles while building a dream castle, yet on a scale to dwarf men. We crawled through tunnels to find in the center of the labyrinth a seawater pool. Sun filtered through chinks overhead to reflect from the bottom, illuminating the cavern's interior with shimmering light. The only comparison that came to mind was the Blue Grotto of Capri.

When we left our anchorage inside the reef of Little Dix Bay, the wind was almost dead aft. Our next goal was a visit to old friends, Louis and Beth Bigelow, on Guana

went down, the sharks moving in for the kill. The same thoughts were racing through Mel's head, for he told me later, "You could almost hear the hoofs pounding the deck!"

Before going over the side, Paul had demonstrated an underwater scream to use if a shark appeared. Sounding rather like the rebel yell of the Confederacy, it had a dual purpose—to warn other swimmers and to turn the creature. Just as my thoughts were most gruesome, I heard the yell. Paul had seen a shark. Had an official timer been present, Olympic records might have fallen as I swam back to the boat!

Paul explained the grisly cargo of the *Rocas* as we returned to the island. "She carried animal bones to be converted to

Like bursting fireworks, a coral bush explodes with color beside a pale yellow pin-wheel, the belladonna. Along with the roselike wild cactus blossom and the delicate frangipani, the plants add swatches of color to the Virgin Islands, a once-fertile volcanic range made barren when early European settlers hacked away the forests and planted sugar cane. After the industry declined more than a century ago, sparse growth crept back. Today, though conservation and reforestation tinge some islands with green, most still remain little more than eroded, scrub-covered rocks.

FRED WARD, BLACK STAR

Island, just off Tortola. I had long been looking forward to revisiting the island, which takes its name from a rock formation that resembles in silhouette the head of the giant lizard called iguana.

Louis and Beth Bigelow long ago had determined to create a paradise of their own on a tropical island. Their search took them first to the South Pacific, but on returning to the West Indies they found Guana and knew it was to be their home. To share it with friends also wanting an island retreat, the Bigelows organized a club of limited membership. Now a central clubhouse stands on the site of an old mansion, while smaller cottages perch on the nearby slopes.

As *Finisterre* sailed in to anchor in White Bay almost exactly where *Carib* had swung, I found the scene unchanged. Low buildings blending into the hillside still rode the saddle between two peaks overlooking the harbor. From the same crescent of powdery sand the variegated colors of the water extended to the Tortola shore.

As I stood talking with the Bigelows after our arrival, a flock of pelicans "pointed" our dinner's first course, as hunting dogs might point game. With a great commotion of flapping wings the ungainly birds gathered from surrounding rocks to crash-dive the shallows. At each splash, the water boiled as small fish tried to escape.

"Hmmm, schools of fry come here in the spring," said Louis. "I hadn't realized it, but I guess they've arrived." Almost simultaneously Beth asked, "Do you like whitebait?"—referring to the English delicacy of crisply fried whole fish, minnow-size, eaten almost like potato chips. Receiving an affirmative answer, she and Louis at once dispatched boys with nets to scoop silver morsels from the water near the beach.

While Louis supervised the netting, we returned to *Finisterre*. I wanted to ghost past the head of the giant iguana at sunset, when the light was perfect for a silhouette. The photographer in Win Parks overcame the sailing enthusiast, and he and Henry cast off in the Whaler to make pictures.

Cove of Trunk Bay curves into St. John, where in 1956 the United States created the Virgin Islands National Park. Nearby, a watery trail guides swimmers through shimmering coral.

The breeze freshened as the sun neared the sea, and Mel and I had a busy few minutes changing jibs. Then the two of us enjoyed a glorious hour as the sun slipped into the horizon and long shadows gathered on the slopes of Tortola. Back and forth we reached, rail down, in one of the truly perfect sails in my memory.

Next morning it was still blowing, and off the Atlantic side of Tortola the sea was rough. But we felt exhilaration as *Finisterre* climbed the back of each tall roller to shoot into the succeeding trough. The wave crests were white, and spray glittered against a cloudless sky. While Tortola unfolded as a series of jutting points and deeply indented bays, Jost Van Dyke loomed ahead.

Before noon we entered Jost Van Dyke's Great Harbour to discover a poignant contrast between land and sea. Although the anchorage was superb, the island was burned dry by the drought. We found that the settlement was almost deserted, for many of its people had left to seek employment elsewhere. The island looked too barren to support a goat. Yet Jost Van Dyke once had been noted for its cattle, and the ruins of a windmill were evidence that this land had produced at least some sugar cane.

We returned to *Finisterre* to swim and to toast with champagne both ship and crew, for our cruise of the beautiful Caribbees was nearing an end.

After a lunch to match the occasion, we got under way smartly, carrying mainsail and small jib. Now the wind was on the beam, even fresher. In a smother of spray we drove for the gap between Congo Cay and Johnson Reef, off the corner of St. John. Suddenly, from the wheel, I became worried to see Henry Davis and Win Parks standing on the bow, scanning the water ahead. Fearful that I had made a mistake in plotting the course, I yelled, "What's wrong? What are you looking for?"

With a laugh Henry called back, "We're watching for the black line that shows on the chart, where we cross from British to U. S. waters."

The sea smoothed as we entered Pillsbury Sound, another of the Virgins' protected waterways, lying between St. Thomas and St. John. A strong head tide met us at the Durloe Cays but the wind remained fresh, driving us through Cruz Bay off St. John, where we formally entered the territorial waters of the United States.

Officially home, we backtracked a mile to Caneel Bay. When I had anchored there in *Carib*, I went over the side to dive for conchs, and explored deserted Trunk Bay, one of the loveliest beaches in the world. Now, cottages and beach-front units invite travelers to Caneel Bay Plantation, a non-profit resort lying within the boundaries of the Virgin Islands National Park—all of this another example of Laurance Rockefeller's continuing endeavors to preserve the beauty of the islands. He donated 5,000 acres to the U. S. Government to found the park now embracing two-thirds of St. John.

Sleek yachts wait off Caneel Bay Plantation, a nonprofit resort established by Laurance S. Rockefeller, who gave the first 5,000 acres for the island park that now covers most of St. John.

Wares from the world over stock the shopping streets of Charlotte Amalie, a free port on St. Thomas. Scandinavian imports fill shelves of the shop above. Islanders enjoy home-grown products—"drinking coconuts" and plantains ready for cooking.

TED SPIEGEL, RAPHO GUILLUMETTE

That evening we dined at the resort with Mel, as our host, and fellow guests Hugh and Jeanne Muller. Hugh, a National Park Service naturalist, gave us a fascinating account of the creation of an underwater nature trail. Skin divers swim along a marked watery path winding through a colorful coral reef, an offshore parkland.

In a rented pink jeep Mel had bounced along rugged hillside roads, and after dinner shared his adventures with us. Near the camping area on Cinnamon Bay, he explored vine-choked ruins of sugar mills recalling the thriving plantations that covered the island 150 years ago.

Following densely forested trails, Mel found old irrigation trenches and a lovely pool with Indian petroglyphs carved in nearby rocks. Who did the work, he wondered, Arawaks or fierce Caribs? Cacao, kapok, and flamboyant trees, hibiscus, sea grapes, and other shrubbery created a tropical paradise.

Next day, *Finisterre* slid across smooth water toward St. Thomas, long a goal of seafarers. As early as 1764 its capital, Charlotte Amalie, was declared a free port by the King of Denmark. It became not only a center of legitimate trade but also, in the words of my 1818 volume of sailing directions, of "such traffic as the French, English, Dutch, and Spaniards dare not carry on publicly in their own islands."

In those days trim black schooners slipped in and out of the same passes we were using, for the Virgins archipelago was one of the favorite haunts of the "Brethren of the Coast"—the pirates. Dominating Charlotte Amalie from a bluff off to the east is Bluebeard Castle, where the pirate by that name supposedly maintained a lookout tower. The place is now a hotel. On another nearby eminence stood the stronghold of Edward Teach, better known as Blackbeard.

Blackbeard was one of the most thorough-going and picturesque rascals in buccaneer history. His whiskers grew so long he braided them. In battle he fired cannon by thrusting slow-burning matches through loops in his beard.

He terrified not only his victims but also his associates. One of his amusements was to create a miniature version of hell aboard

203

his ship by battening down the hatches and igniting sulphur in the hold; he then led his crew down to see who could take it longest. Legend has it he always won, for there were those who believed he was the devil incarnate—until his head finally decorated the bowsprit of a Royal Navy sloop in Carolina waters.

As *Finisterre* crept slowly into the harbor of Charlotte Amalie, a sloop from Tortola paralleled our course. Its deck was piled with produce, and a goat was tethered to the mainmast. Here remains one of the last strongholds of commercial sail. Along Veterans Drive where the schooners berth, the strong sweet smell of rum in casks blends with the rich aroma of coffee, as cargoes from all the West Indies are unloaded, and dusky sailors sing as they add patches to crazy-quilt sails.

Nearing the steamer-turning basin, both the Tortola sloop and *Finisterre* had to change course to avoid the monster bow of a passenger liner towering high above

Lights of Charlotte Amalie star the darkening hills around Yacht Haven, where Finisterre *moored off U. S.-owned St. Thomas at the end of the island cruise.*

our mainmast. For Charlotte Amalie is also an international crossroads, still a free port. Freighters and cruise ships load and discharge in their own section of the magnificent port, yet leave a sanctuary for the small cruising yacht.

As I turned our bow toward Yacht Haven and its cluster of masts and waving burgees, I looked over my shoulder at Charlotte Amalie, now open before us. Houses covered the slopes of three low hills—Government, Berg, and French on modern maps but called Foretop, Maintop, and Mizzentop in windjammer days.

Some streets were too steep for paving, so they remained flights of steps. Somehow for me this port, looking out across a sheltered anchorage to the horizon of the Caribbean, was a true sailor's town, symbolizing the sailor's duality: love of the water, but need for the land, with an alternate desire to escape from each.

Now it was our turn to be ashore for a while. The Isles of the Caribbees lay astern.

Index

Illustrations references appear in *italics*.

Composition by National Geographic's Phototypographic Division, Herman J. A. C. Arens, Director; Robert C. Ellis, Jr., Manager
Printed and bound by Fawcett-Haynes Printing Corporation, Rockville, Md.
Color separations by Lanman Engraving Company, Alexandria, Va.; Beck Engraving Company, Philadelphia, Pa.; and Graphic Color Plate, Inc., Stamford, Conn.

TEÂTRE de la GUERRE en AMERIQUE telle qu'elle est à present Possedée par les ESPAGNO